LEARNING TARGETS
for Literacy

Fiction and Poetry Years 3 and 4

Key Stage 2 Scotland P4–P5

Wendy Wren

Stanley Thornes (Publishers) Ltd

Acknowledgments

The author and publishers wish to thank the following for permission to use copyright material:

Andersen Press Ltd for material from Melvin Burgess, *The Earth Giant* (1995) pp. 48–51; John Cotton for 'First Things'; Egmont Children's Books for material from Garry Kilworth, *The Gargoyle*, Mammoth (1997) pp. 14–18; Anne English for 'Birds in the Garden'; Faber and Faber Ltd for material from Margaret Joy, 'Jeremy the Jerbil' from *Allotment Lane School Again* (1985) 7–12; and Judith Nicholls, 'Storytime' from *Midnight Forest*; Folens Publishers Ltd UK for 'Firecracker' from *The Essential Guide to Poetry* (1992). Copyright © Folens Publishers Ltd UK; HarperCollins Publishers Ltd for material from C. S. Lewis, *The Lion, the Witch and the Wardrobe* (1974) pp. 11–14; David Higham Associates on behalf of the authors for Charles Causley, 'I Saw a Jolly Hunter' from *Collected Poems*; Bel Mooney,'A Child's Cry' from *The Stove Haunting* (1996) pp. 33–5; Richard Adams, *Watership Down*, Penguin; and Berlie Doherty, 'White Water' from *Walking on Air*, HarperCollins Publishers; International Thomson Publishing Company for material from Bernie Wade, Ann Wade and Maggie Moore, 'Watch What You Say' from *Around the World*, Story Chest, Thomas Nelson and Sons Ltd (1986); Penguin Books Ltd for material from Joy Allen, *Teeth for Charlie* (Hamish Hamilton, 1976) pp. 5–9. Copyright © 1976 Joy Allen; and Jean Ure, *The Phantom Knicker Nicker* (Blackie, 1993) pp. 5–10. Copyright © Jean Ure, 1993; Jennifer Luithlen Agency on behalf of the author for Robert Swindells, *The World-Eater* (1991), Hodder & Stoughton Children's Books (1991) pp. 11–14, and Doubleday UK; Peters, Fraser & Dunlop Group Ltd on behalf of the author for Roger McGough, 'First Haiku of Spring'; Random House UK Ltd for Francis Scarfe, 'Cats' from *Underworlds*, William Heinemann; Rogers, Coleridge and White Ltd on behalf of the author for Gareth Owen, 'Conversation Piece', first published in *Salford Road*, Young Lions (1988); Vernon Scannell for 'Jason's Trial' (1996); Caroline Sheldon Literacy Agency on behalf of the author for John Agard, 'Cat in the Dark'; The Society of Authors as the Literacy Representatives of the Estates of the authors for James Stephens, 'The Snare'; Richard le Gallienne, 'I Meant To Do My Work Today'; and an excerpt from John Masefield, 'Reynard the Fox'.

Every effort has been made to trace the copyright holders but if any have been inadvertently overlooked the publishers will be pleased to make the necessary arrangements at the earliest opportunity.

First published in 1999 by
Stanley Thornes Publishers Ltd
Ellenborough House
Wellington Street
Cheltenham GL50 1YW

99 00 01 02 03 / 10 9 8 7 6 5 4 3 2 1

A catalogue record for this book is available from the British Library.

ISBN 0-7487-3600-X

Typeset by Tech-Set, Gateshead, Tyne & Wear
Edited by Angela Wigmore, Cheltenham, Gloucestershire
Illustrations by Debbie Clarke
Printed and bound in Great Britain by Redwood Books, Trowbridge, Wiltshire

CONTENTS

Welcome to Learning Targets iv
Introduction vi
Scottish Guidelines planner vii

SECTION 1
Year 3 Term 1 **1**
National Literacy Strategy planner 2
UNIT **1** Story settings 3
UNIT **2** Dialogue 9
UNIT **3** Poetry writing 18

SECTION 2
Year 3 Term 2 **25**
National Literacy Strategy planner 26
UNIT **1** Traditional stories 27
UNIT **2** Characters 31
UNIT **3** Story plans 37

SECTION 3
Year 3 Term 3 **45**
National Literacy Strategy planner 46
UNIT **1** Story openings 47
UNIT **2** First person accounts 54
UNIT **3** Fact and fiction 60
UNIT **4** Playing with language 63

SECTION 4
Year 4 Term 1 **70**
National Literacy Strategy planner 71
UNIT **1** Characters 72
UNIT **2** Play scripts 77
UNIT **3** Poetry writing 85

SECTION 5
Year 4 Term 2 **93**
National Literacy Strategy planner 94
UNIT **1** Creating imaginary worlds 95
UNIT **2** Poems from long ago 101
UNIT **3** Editing 106

SECTION 6
Year 4 Term 3 **114**
National Literacy Strategy planner 115
UNIT **1** Stories raising issues 116
UNIT **2** Poetry forms 121
UNIT **3** Syllabic poetry 127

Welcome to LEARNING TARGETS

Learning Targets is a series of practical teacher's resource books written to help you to plan and deliver well-structured, professional lessons in line with all the relevant curriculum documents.

Each Learning Target book provides exceptionally clear lesson plans that cover the whole of its stated curriculum plus a large bank of carefully structured copymasters. Links to the key curriculum documents are provided throughout to enable you to plan effectively.

The Learning Targets series has been written in response to the challenge confronting teachers not just to come up with teaching ideas which cover the curriculum but to ensure that they deliver high quality lessons every lesson with the emphasis on raising standards of pupil achievement.

The recent thinking from OFSTED, and the National Literacy and Numeracy Strategies on the key factors in effective teaching has been built into the structure of Learning Targets. These might briefly be summarised as follows:

- that effective teaching is active teaching directed to very clear objectives
- that good lessons are delivered with pace, rigour and purpose
- that good teaching requires a range of strategies - including interactive whole class sessions
- that ongoing formative assessment is essential to plan children's learning
- that differentiation is necessary but that it must be realistic.

The emphasis in Learning Targets is on absolute clarity. We have written and designed the books to enable you to access and deliver effective lessons as easily as possible, with the following aims:

- to plan and deliver rigorous, well-structured lessons
- to set explicit targets for achievement in every lesson that you teach
- to make the children aware of what they are going to learn
- to put the emphasis on direct, active teaching every time
- to make effective use of time and resources
- to employ the full range of recommended strategies whole-class, group and individual work
- to differentiate for ability groups realistically
- to use ongoing formative assessment to plan your next step
- to have ready access to usable pupil copymasters to support your teaching.

The page opposite provides an at-a-glance guide to the key features of the Learning Targets lessons and explains how they will enable you deliver effective lessons. The key to symbols on the lesson plans is set out here. ➤➝

How to deliver structured lessons with pace, rigour and purpose

Explicit targets for achievement in every lesson

The concise subject knowledge you need

Crystal clear lesson plan layouts

The full range of teaching strategies

Rigorous and practical activities

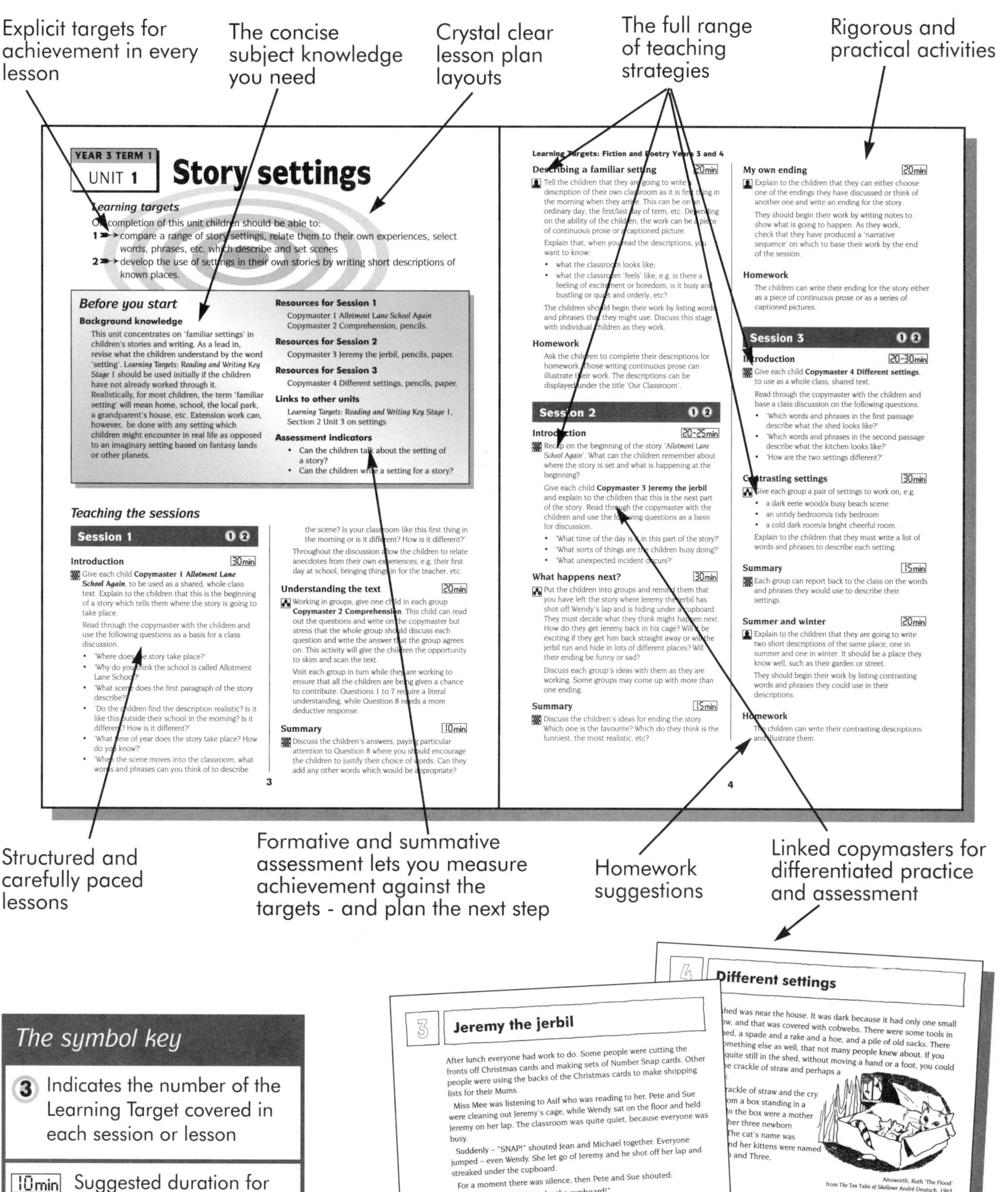

YEAR 3 TERM 1
UNIT 1

Story settings

Learning targets

On completion of this unit children should be able to:

1 ➤ compare a range of story settings, relate them to their own experiences, select words, phrases, etc. which describe and set scenes

2 ➤ develop the use of settings in their own stories by writing short descriptions of known places.

Before you start

Background knowledge

This unit concentrates on 'familiar settings' in children's stories and writing. As a lead in, revise what the children understand by the word 'setting'. *Learning Targets: Reading and Writing Key Stage 1* should be used initially if the children have not already worked through it.
Realistically, for most children, the term 'familiar setting' will mean home, school, the local park, a grandparent's house, etc. Extension work can, however, be done with any setting which children might encounter in real life as opposed to an imaginary setting based on fantasy lands or other planets.

Resources for Session 1

Copymaster 1 *Allotment Lane School Again*
Copymaster 2 Comprehension, pencils.

Resources for Session 2

Copymaster 3 Jeremy the jerbil, pencils, paper.

Resources for Session 3

Copymaster 4 Different settings, pencils, paper.

Links to other units

Learning Targets: Reading and Writing Key Stage 1, Section 2 Unit 3 on settings

Assessment indicators

- Can the children talk about the setting of a story?
- Can the children write a setting for a story?

Teaching the sessions

Session 1 ① ②

Introduction 30min

Give each child **Copymaster 1 *Allotment Lane School Again***, to be used as a shared, whole class text. Explain to the children that this is the beginning of a story which tells them where the story is going to take place.

Read through the copymaster with the children and use the following questions as a basis for a class discussion.

- 'Where does the story take place?'
- 'Why do you think the school is called Allotment Lane School?'
- 'What scene does the first paragraph of the story describe?'
- 'Do the children find the description realistic? Is it like this outside their school in the morning? Is it different? How is it different?'
- 'What time of year does the story take place? How do you know?'
- 'When the scene moves into the classroom, what words and phrases can you think of to describe the scene? Is your classroom like this first thing in the morning or is it different? How is it different?'

Throughout the discussion allow the children to relate anecdotes from their own experiences, e.g. their first day at school, bringing things in for the teacher, etc.

Understanding the text 20min

Working in groups, give one child in each group **Copymaster 2 Comprehension**. This child can read out the questions and write on the copymaster but stress that the whole group should discuss each question and write the answer that the group agrees on. This activity will give the children the opportunity to skim and scan the text.

Visit each group in turn while they are working to ensure that all the children are being given a chance to contribute. Questions 1 to 7 require a literal understanding, while Question 8 needs a more deductive response.

Summary 10min

Discuss the children's answers, paying particular attention to Question 8 where you should encourage the children to justify their choice of words. Can they add any other words which would be appropriate?

3

Learning Targets: Fiction and Poetry Years 3 and 4

Describing a familiar setting 20min

Tell the children that they are going to write a description of their own classroom as it is first thing in the morning when they arrive. This can be on an ordinary day, the first/last day of term, etc. Depending on the ability of the children, the work can be a piece of continuous prose or a captioned picture.

Explain that, when you read the descriptions, you want to know:

- what the classroom looks like;
- what the classroom 'feels' like, e.g. is there a feeling of excitement or boredom; is it busy and bustling or quiet and orderly, etc?

The children should begin their work by listing words and phrases that they might use. Discuss this stage with individual children as they work.

Homework

Ask the children to complete their descriptions for homework. Those writing continuous prose can illustrate their work. The descriptions can be displayed under the title 'Our Classroom'.

Session 2 ① ②

Introduction 20–25min

Recap on the beginning of the story '*Allotment Lane School Again*'. What can the children remember about where the story is set and what is happening at the beginning?

Give each child **Copymaster 3 Jeremy the jerbil** and explain to the children that this is the next part of the story. Read through the copymaster with the children and use the following questions as a basis for discussion.

- 'What time of the day is it in this part of the story?'
- 'What sorts of things are the children busy doing?'
- 'What unexpected incident occurs?'

What happens next? 30min

Put the children into groups and remind them that you have left the story where Jeremy the jerbil has shot off Wendy's lap and is hiding under a cupboard. They must decide what they think might happen next. How do they get Jeremy back in his cage? Will it be exciting if they get him back straight away or will the jerbil run and hide in lots of different places? Will their ending be funny or sad?

Discuss each group's ideas with them as they are working. Some groups may come up with more than one ending.

Summary 15min

Discuss the children's ideas for ending the story. Which one is the favourite? Which do they think is the funniest, the most realistic, etc?

My own ending 20min

Explain to the children that they can either choose one of the endings they have discussed or think of another one and write an ending for the story.

They should begin their work by writing notes to show what is going to happen. As they work, check that they have produced a 'narrative sequence' on which to base their work by the end of the session.

Homework

The children can write their ending for the story either as a piece of continuous prose or as a series of captioned pictures.

Session 3 ① ②

Introduction 20–30min

Give each child **Copymaster 4 Different settings**, to use as a whole class, shared text.

Read through the copymaster with the children and base a class discussion on the following questions.

- 'Which words and phrases in the first passage describe what the shed looks like?'
- 'Which words and phrases in the second passage describe what the kitchen looks like?'
- 'How are the two settings different?'

Contrasting settings 30min

Give each group a pair of settings to work on, e.g.

- a dark eerie wood/a busy beach scene
- an untidy bedroom/a tidy bedroom
- a cold dark room/a bright cheerful room.

Explain to the children that they must write a list of words and phrases to describe each setting.

Summary 15min

Each group can report back to the class on the words and phrases they would use to describe their settings.

Summer and winter 20min

Explain to the children that they are going to write two short descriptions of the same place, one in summer and one in winter. It should be a place they know well, such as their garden or street.

They should begin their work by listing contrasting words and phrases they could use in their descriptions.

Homework

The children can write their contrasting descriptions and illustrate them.

4

Structured and carefully paced lessons

Formative and summative assessment lets you measure achievement against the targets - and plan the next step

Homework suggestions

Linked copymasters for differentiated practice and assessment

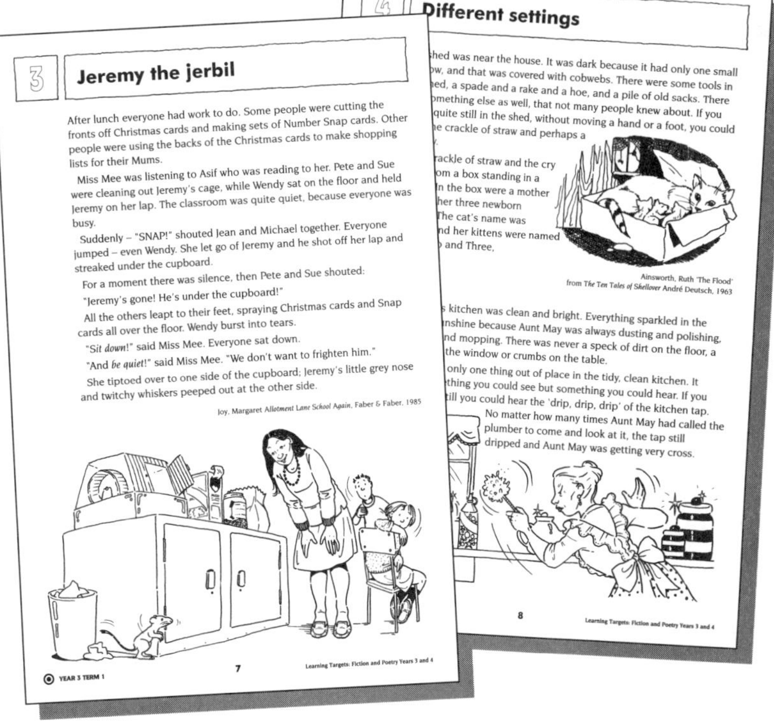

3 **Jeremy the jerbil**

After lunch everyone had work to do. Some people were cutting the fronts off Christmas cards and making sets of Number Snap cards. Other people were using the backs of the Christmas cards to make shopping lists for their Mums.

Miss Mee was listening to Asif who was reading to her. Pete and Sue were cleaning out Jeremy's cage, while Wendy sat on the floor and held Jeremy on her lap. The classroom was quite quiet, because everyone was busy.

Suddenly – "SNAP!" shouted Jean and Michael together. Everyone jumped – even Wendy. She let go of Jeremy and he shot off her lap and streaked under the cupboard.

For a moment there was silence, then Pete and Sue shouted:

"Jeremy's gone! He's under the cupboard!"

All the others leapt to their feet, spraying Christmas cards and Snap cards all over the floor. Wendy burst into tears.

"*Sit down!*" said Miss Mee. Everyone sat down.

"*And be quiet!*" said Miss Mee. "We don't want to frighten him."

She tiptoed over to one side of the cupboard; Jeremy's little grey nose and twitchy whiskers peeped out at the other side.

Joy, Margaret *Allotment Lane School Again*, Faber & Faber, 1985

YEAR 3 TERM 1 7 Learning Targets: Fiction and Poetry Years 3 and 4

4 **Different settings**

...hed was near the house. It was dark because it had only one small ...w, and that was covered with cobwebs. There were some tools in ...ed, a spade and a rake and a hoe, and a pile of old sacks. There ...mething else as well, that not many people knew about. If you ...quite still in the shed, without moving a hand or a foot, you could ...e crackle of straw and perhaps a ...

...rackle of straw and the cry ...om a box standing in a ...n the box were a mother ...her three newborn ...he cat's name was ...d her kittens were named ... and Three.

Ainsworth, Ruth 'The Flood' from *The Ten Tales of Shellover* André Deutsch, 1963

...kitchen was clean and bright. Everything sparkled in the ...nshine because Aunt May was always dusting and polishing, ...nd mopping. There was never a speck of dirt on the floor, a ...the window or crumbs on the table.

...only one thing out of place in the tidy, clean kitchen. It ...thing you could see but something you could hear. If you ...ill you could hear the 'drip, drip, drip' of the kitchen tap. No matter how many times Aunt May had called the plumber to come and look at it, the tap still dripped and Aunt May was getting very cross.

8 Learning Targets: Fiction and Poetry Years 3 and 4

The symbol key

③	Indicates the number of the Learning Target covered in each session or lesson
10min	Suggested duration for each part of the session
[A]	Assessment opportunity
[interactive whole class symbol]	Interactive whole class teaching session
[group symbol]	Group work session
[pair symbol]	Pair work session
[individual symbol]	Individual session

INTRODUCTION

Learning Targets for Literacy: Fiction and Poetry Years 3 and 4 provides detailed coverage of comprehension and composition level work for English for fiction and poetry. Together with the accompanying book *Non-fiction Years 3 and 4*, it provides an invaluable resource for text level work for the National Literacy Strategy and for Scotland P4–P5. The two other Learning Targets books at Key Stage 2, *Grammar and Punctuation* and *Spelling*, cover sentence and word level work respectively.

This book covers reading and writing fiction and poetry at the level of the text: how to read, understand and write all the relevant genres at Years 3 and 4. All the related decoding, spelling, handwriting and grammar skills for Key Stage 2 are covered in the other two books at this level.

This book is not, of course, a complete literacy scheme. It cannot provide you with all the resources needed to deliver text level literacy for fiction and poetry to your class. It is, however, a highly comprehensive resource book which covers all the main requirements through a series of well-structured, detailed and specific lesson plans backed by linked copymasters that provide you with both pupil sheets and photocopiable anthology materials that give you the reading materials you need to deliver the lessons.

How this book is organised

The sections

This book is divided into six sections. Each one covers one term's work in Years 3 and 4 for the National Literacy Strategy and closely follows the range of work and the detailed plans for fiction and poetry on pages 32–43 of the National Literacy Strategy document. Each section begins with a short overview of the term's work and provides assessment objectives linked to copymasters. A National Literacy Strategy planner is also included at this point.

The units

Sections are sub-divided into units. Each unit is an integrated piece of work which combines reading and writing skills to meet particular learning targets. These learning targets state explicitly what the children should aim to know or be able to do by the end of the unit and provide you with a set of clear, assessable objectives to teach any lesson on reading and writing fiction and poetry at text level.

Together, the units in a section form an overall set of lesson plans to cover the term's work. They are 'free-standing' so that in Section 1 Year 3 Term 1 you can, for example, use Unit 2 on dialogue to meet a particular objective within your teaching programme without having undertaken Unit 1 on story settings. In general, units at the beginning of a section are easier and difficulty builds up incrementally to a mastery of the assessment objectives outlined at the start. Children's progress can be summatively assessed using the assessment copymasters at the end of the section.

The sessions

Units are composed of a number of teaching 'sessions'. These teaching suggestions are very specific and detailed, and use the full range of teaching strategies required during the literacy hour: teacher-directed whole class work, individual, pair and group work. Approximate times are suggested to enable you to fit the sessions into your literacy hour programme. In practice, of course, the times actually required will vary according to the children's ability and the way the sessions are going. You will find a key to the symbols used in the sessions on page *v*.

Within a unit, the sessions tend to increase in complexity. Particular sessions may be used independently of the overall unit for a particular purpose but the sessions within a unit are closely linked, being designed to provide a teaching programme which combines reading and writing fiction and poetry with best practice in teaching literacy skills. You will probably want to teach the sessions within the context of their whole units.

The copymasters

Photocopiable sheets can be found at the end of every unit and these are integral to teaching the sessions. As well as providing activities and information, they also include extracts, anthology materials and assessment sheets. Although a book of this kind cannot provide all the reading materials required to deliver the Strategy, it should not be necessary to seek out many extra resources to deliver the targeted literacy objectives. All the coymasters are reinforced by structured lesson plans.

Using this book alongside The National Literacy Strategy and the Scottish Guidelines.

You will find a National Literacy Strategy planner for each term's work after the Section introduction . This details the term's work and shows where you can find units and sessions to resource it. You will find that the learning targets closely follow the content and wording of the fiction and poetry requirements for Years 3 and 4 in the National Literacy Strategy document.

Each unit of work can supply the material for a string of literacy hours. Units can be broken up into their constituent sessions across the week, using the timings as an approximate guide. Many of the activities and sessions can be used very flexibly and differentiation within the sessions is as much by outcome as by activity. Every teacher will, of course, interpret the demands of the literacy hour individually in the light of their own situation.

Despite its Literacy Strategy structure, all the ideas in the book are equally applicable to the Scottish situation: they are, in essence, structured and effective ideas for good practice in literacy teaching in all situations. You will find an outline planner linking the book to the Scottish English Language 5–14 Guidelines on the next page.

Scottish Guidelines planner

For teachers in Scotland, we have mapped the overall contents of the book against the attainment targets at Levels B–D, with occasional reference to Level E, for reading and writing. Necessarily a very wide range of attainment can often be covered by any one session, unit or section. The correlation's below are for general guidance only. Because this book focuses on fiction and poetry, awareness of a wide range of genres is not a key feature. The key writing focus is very much on imaginative writing.

Reading

Reading for enjoyment

Level B: Read stories, poems regularly for enjoyment: Sections 1–3.
Level C: Read regularly for enjoyment and give an opinion on texts of different kinds: Sections 1–6.
Level D: Read regularly for enjoyment texts with a range of subject matter and, with some support, reflect on what has been read and record personal reactions: Sections 3–6.

Reading to reflect on the writer's ideas and craft.

Level B: Read straightforward texts and in discussion and writing show that they understand the main ideas: Sections 1–3.

Level C: Read a variety of straightforward texts, and in discussion and writing show that they understand the main and supporting ideas, and can draw conclusions from the text where appropriate: Sections 1–6.

Level D: Read a variety of texts, and in discussion and writing show that they understand the gist of the text, its main ideas and/or feelings, and can obtain particular information: and comment on the simpler aspects of the writer's craft: Sections 3–6.

Awareness of genre (type of text)

Level B: Show recognition of a few features of different types of simple texts: stories, poems, dramatic texts: all sections.

Level C: Identify a few obvious features of form and content in different types of text: stories, poems, dramatic texts: all sections.

Level D: Identify some similarities and differences of form and content in examples of the same type of text: Sections 4–6.

Knowledge about language

Level B: Show that they know, understand and can use at least the following terms: author, character, setting the scene, poem: Section 1, Units 1–3; Section 2, Unit 1; Section 3, Unit 1; Section 4, Unit 1; Section 6, Unit 2.

Level C: Show that they know, understand and can use at least the following terms: fiction, plot, dialogue, main character, conflict: Section 1, Unit 2; Section 2, Units 2, 3; Section 3, Unit 1; Section 4, Unit 1; Section 5, Unit 1; Section 6, Unit 1.

Level D: Show that they know, understand and can use at least the following terms: theme, character, relationships, setting, motives: Section 1, Units 1, 2; Section 2, Units 1-3; Section 3, Units 1, 3; Section 4, Unit 1; Section 5, Unit 1; Section 6, Unit 1.

Level E: Show that they know, understand and can use at least the following terms: syllable, simile, metaphor: Section 5, Units 1, 2; Section 6, Unit 2.

Writing

Personal writing

Level B: Write briefly and in an appropriate sequence about a personal experience, giving an indication of feelings, using adequate vocabulary: Section 1, Unit 1; Section 3, Unit 3; Section 4, Unit 1.

Level C: Write about a personal experience for a specific purpose and audience, using appropriate organisation and vocabulary: Section 3, Unit 3; Section 4, Unit 1.

Level D: Write about personal experiences, expressing thoughts and feelings for a specific purpose and audience and using appropriate organisation and vocabulary: Section 4, Unit 1.

Imaginative writing

Level B: Write a brief, imaginative story or poem or dialogue with discernible organisation and using adequate vocabulary: Section 1, Units, 1–3; Section 2, Units 1–3.

Level C: Write a brief, imaginative story, poem or play, using appropriate organisation and vocabulary: Section 1, Units 1, 3; Section 2, Units 1–3; Section 3, Units 1–3; Section 4, Units 1–3.

Level D: Write imaginative pieces in various genres, using appropriate organisation and vocabulary: Section 3, Units 1–3; Section 4, Units 1–3; Section 5, Units 1, 2; Section 6 Units 1–3.

Level E: Write imaginative pieces in various genres, making some use of appropriate literary conventions: Section 4, Units 1–3; Section 5, Units 1, 2; Section 6, Units 1–3.

YEAR 3 TERM 1

Focus

In this section children will be given the opportunity to:

1 investigate/write familiar settings for stories

2 investigate/write dialogue in stories

3 investigate/write simple play scripts based on stories

4 investigate/write simple poetry, e.g. shape poems.

Content

Unit 1: Story settings
Unit 2: Dialogue
Unit 3: Poetry writing

Reading List

Agard, John 'Cat in the Dark' from *My Red Poetry Book*, Macmillan, 1988

Ainsworth, Ruth 'The Flood', from *A Sackful of Stories for Eight Year Olds*, Corgi Books, 1992

Allen, Joy *Teeth for Charlie*, Hamish Hamilton, 1976

Joy, Margaret *Allotment Lane School Again*, Faber & Faber, 1985

Scarfe, Francis 'Cats' from *Poems for 9-Year-Olds and Under*, Puffin, 1985

The Essential Guide to Poetry, Folens Publishers Ltd UK, 1992

Ure, Jean *The Phantom Knicker Nicker*, Blackie, 1993

Assessment

Assessment Copymasters 12–14 are at the end of the section.

Copymaster 12 Stories with familiar settings

Reading comprehension: literal and inferential comprehension within a familiar setting.

Writing composition: ask the children to choose one of the following titles and write a description that they could use as a setting for a story: 'My Garden' or 'The Supermarket'.

Copymaster 13 Plays

Writing composition: this copymaster gives the children the opportunity to convert a passage from a story into a play script.

Copymaster 14 Poetry

Reading comprehension: literal and inferential comprehension of a rhyming poem.

Writing composition: the children can choose one of the following titles and write a shape poem about it: 'The Snake' or 'Using a Spade'.

National Literacy Strategy planner

This chart shows you how to find activities by unit to resource your term's requirements for text level work on fiction and poetry. The Learning Targets closely follow the structure of the fiction and poetry requirements for the term in the National Literacy Strategy document (pages 32–33). A few of the requirements are not covered. These are usually the ones that require extended reading or writing or comparison of several different texts.

YEAR 3 TERM 1

Range

Fiction and poetry:

- stories with familiar settings
- plays
- poems based on observation and the senses
- shape poems.

TEXT LEVEL WORK

COMPREHENSION AND COMPOSITION

Reading comprehension

Pupils should be taught:

1 to compare a range of story settings, and to select words and phrases that describe scenes: Unit 1;

2 how dialogue is presented in stories, e.g. through statements, questions, exclamations; how paragraphing is used to organise dialogue: Unit 2;

3 to be aware of the different voices in stories using dramatised readings, showing differences between the narrator and different characters used, e.g. puppets to present stories: Unit 2;

4 to read, prepare and present play scripts: Unit 2;

5 to recognise the key differences between prose and play script, e.g. by looking at dialogue, stage directions, layout of text in prose and play scripts: Unit 2;

6 to read aloud and recite poems, comparing different views of the same subject; to discuss choice of words and phrases that describe and create impact, e.g. adjectives, powerful and expressive verbs, e.g. 'stare' instead of 'look': Unit 3;

7 to distinguish between rhyming and non-rhyming poetry and comment on the impact of layout: Unit 3;

8 to express their views about a story or poem, identifying specific words and phrases to support their viewpoint: Unit 1;

Writing composition

Pupils should be taught:

9 to generate ideas relevant to a topic by brainstorming, word association, etc: Units 1–3;

10 using reading as a model, to write own passages of dialogue: Unit 2;

11 to develop the use of settings in own stories by:

- writing short descriptions of known places
- by writing a description in the style of a familiar story
- to investigate and collect sentences/phrases for story openings and endings – use some of these formal elements in re-telling and story writing: Unit1;

12 to collect stuitable words and phrases, in order to write poems and short descriptions; design simple patterns with words, use repetitive phrases; write imaginative comparisons: Unit 3;

13 to invent calligrams and a range of shape poems, selecting appropriate words and careful presentation; build up class collections: Unit3;

14 to write simple play scripts based on own reading and oral work: Unit 2;

15 to begin to organise stories into paragraphs; to begin to use paragraphing in presentation of dialogue in stories.

YEAR 3 TERM 1

UNIT **1**

Story settings

Learning targets

On completion of this unit children should be able to:

1 ➤ compare a range of story settings, relate them to their own experiences, select words, phrases, etc. which describe and set scenes

2 ➤ develop the use of settings in their own stories by writing short descriptions of known places.

Before you start

Background knowledge

This unit concentrates on 'familiar settings' in children's stories and writing. As a lead in, revise what the children understand by the word 'setting'. *Learning Targets: Reading and Writing Key Stage* 1 should be used initially if the children have not already worked through it.

Realistically, for most children, the term 'familiar setting' will mean home, school, the local park, a grandparent's house, etc. Extension work can, however, be done with any setting which children might encounter in real life as opposed to an imaginary setting based on fantasy lands or other planets.

Resources for Session 1

Copymaster 1 *Allotment Lane School Again*
Copymaster 2 Comprehension, pencils.

Resources for Session 2

Copymaster 3 Jeremy the jerbil, pencils, paper.

Resources for Session 3

Copymaster 4 Different settings, pencils, paper.

Links to other units

Learning Targets: Reading and Writing Key Stage 1, Section 2 Unit 3 on settings

Assessment indicators

- Can the children talk about the setting of a story?
- Can the children write a setting for a story?

Teaching the sessions

Session 1

Introduction 30 min

Give each child **Copymaster 1 *Allotment Lane School Again***, to be used as a shared, whole class text. Explain to the children that this is the beginning of a story which tells them where the story is going to take place.

Read through the copymaster with the children and use the following questions as a basis for a class discussion.

- 'Where does the story take place?'
- 'Why do you think the school is called Allotment Lane School?'
- 'What scene does the first paragraph of the story describe?'
- 'Do the children find the description realistic? Is it like this outside their school in the morning? Is it different? How is it different?'
- 'What time of year does the story take place? How do you know?'
- 'When the scene moves into the classroom, what words and phrases can you think of to describe the scene? Is your classroom like this first thing in the morning or is it different? How is it different?'

Throughout the discussion allow the children to relate anecdotes from their own experiences, e.g. their first day at school, bringing things in for the teacher, etc.

Understanding the text 20 min

Working in groups, give one child in each group **Copymaster 2 Comprehension**. This child can read out the questions and write on the copymaster but stress that the whole group should discuss each question and write the answer that the group agrees on. This activity will give the children the opportunity to skim and scan the text.

Visit each group in turn while they are working to ensure that all the children are being given a chance to contribute. Questions 1 to 7 require a literal understanding, while Question 8 needs a more deductive response.

Summary 10 min

Discuss the children's answers, paying particular attention to Question 8 where you should encourage the children to justify their choice of words. Can they add any other words which would be appropriate?

Describing a familiar setting

Tell the children that they are going to write a description of their own classroom as it is first thing in the morning when they arrive. This can be on an ordinary day, the first/last day of term, etc. Depending on the ability of the children, the work can be a piece of continuous prose or a captioned picture.

Explain that, when you read the descriptions, you want to know:

- what the classroom looks like;
- what the classroom 'feels' like, e.g. is there a feeling of excitement or boredom; is it busy and bustling or quiet and orderly, etc?

The children should begin their work by listing words and phrases that they might use. Discuss this stage with individual children as they work.

Homework

Ask the children to complete their descriptions for homework. Those writing continuous prose can illustrate their work. The descriptions can be displayed under the title 'Our Classroom'.

Session 2

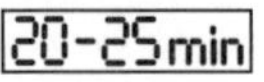

Introduction

20-25min

Recap on the beginning of the story '*Allotment Lane School Again*'. What can the children remember about where the story is set and what is happening at the beginning?

Give each child **Copymaster 3 Jeremy the jerbil** and explain to the children that this is the next part of the story. Read through the copymaster with the children and use the following questions as a basis for discussion.

- 'What time of the day is it in this part of the story?'
- 'What sorts of things are the children busy doing?'
- 'What unexpected incident occurs?'

What happens next?

30min

Put the children into groups and remind them that you have left the story where Jeremy the jerbil has shot off Wendy's lap and is hiding under a cupboard. They must decide what they think might happen next. How do they get Jeremy back in his cage? Will it be exciting if they get him back straight away or will the jerbil run and hide in lots of different places? Will their ending be funny or sad?

Discuss each group's ideas with them as they are working. Some groups may come up with more than one ending.

Summary

15min

Discuss the children's ideas for ending the story. Which one is the favourite? Which do they think is the funniest, the most realistic, etc?

My own ending

Explain to the children that they can either choose one of the endings they have discussed or think of another one and write an ending for the story.

They should begin their work by writing notes to show what is going to happen. As they work, check that they have produced a 'narrative sequence' on which to base their work by the end of the session.

Homework

The children can write their ending for the story either as a piece of continuous prose or as a series of captioned pictures.

Session 3

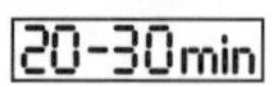

Introduction

20-30min

Give each child **Copymaster 4 Different settings**, to use as a whole class, shared text.

Read through the copymaster with the children and base a class discussion on the following questions.

- 'Which words and phrases in the first passage describe what the shed looks like?'
- 'Which words and phrases in the second passage describe what the kitchen looks like?'
- 'How are the two settings different?'

Contrasting settings

30min

Give each group a pair of settings to work on, e.g.

- a dark eerie wood/a busy beach scene
- an untidy bedroom/a tidy bedroom
- a cold dark room/a bright cheerful room.

Explain to the children that they must write a list of words and phrases to describe each setting.

Summary

15min

Each group can report back to the class on the words and phrases they would use to describe their settings.

Summer and winter

20min

Explain to the children that they are going to write two short descriptions of the same place, one in summer and one in winter. It should be a place they know well, such as their garden or street.

They should begin their work by listing contrasting words and phrases they could use in their descriptions.

Homework

The children can write their contrasting descriptions and illustrate them.

1 Allotment Lane School Again

The Christmas holidays were over. Mr Loftus, the caretaker, unlocked the gates of Allotment Lane School again, ready for the new term. Soon there were crowds of children coming up the lane. Some were with friends, some were with big brothers or sisters, some were helping their mothers with pushchairs. Some were just wandering up the lane on their own, having a little think.

Michael was glad to get back to school. He hung up his coat and ran into the classroom. He was carrying a large carrier bag.

"These are for you," he said, dumping the bag on Miss Mee's chair. "They're from my Gran. She says you can have them – she gets fed up with dusting round them."

Miss Mee looked into the bag.

"Christmas cards!" she said. "Thank you, Michael, we'll make something with them."

Then Laura came in.

"I got a Sindy doll for Christmas," she said. "And my Mum says you can have these Christmas cards." She put a bundle on Miss Mee's table.

"Oh, thank you, Laura," said Miss Mee. "They'll come in very useful."

Then the twins came in with their Dad. He was carrying the jerbil cage; the twins had been looking after Jeremy, the class jerbil, through the Christmas holidays.

"Morning, Miss Mee," said the twins' Dad, putting the cage down on a side table. "We've enjoyed having Jeremy very much, but we ran out of sawdust and straw, I'm afraid, so he needs cleaning out."

"Yes, we'll do that today," said Miss Mee. 'Thank you very much for looking after him."

"We've brought our old Christmas cards to school too," said Rosemary.

"We took them down yesterday and we don't want them any more," said Barbara, the other twin.

"Great," said Miss Mee. "I'm sure we'll find them useful."

Next, Brenda came in. She was carrying a big carrier bag.

"Guess what I've got for you," she said to Miss Mee.

"Christmas cards?" said Miss Mee. Brenda looked puzzled.

"No, of course not," she said. "It's something for Jeremy. It's cardboard rolls. Can I give him one straight away?"

"Yes, all right," said Miss Mee. "He likes one of those to start the day."

They all gathered round and watched. Jeremy sat on his back legs and held the cardboard roll steady with his front paws. He nibbled so fast they couldn't see his teeth – they could only see his nose and whiskers twitching as he bit off little scraps of cardboard.

"He's not eating it," said Michael.

"No, he just likes nibbling," said Laura.

"And he makes a pile of soft scraps to make a den in," said Rosemary.

From *Allotment Lane School Again* by Margaret Joy

2 Comprehension

1 Who is Mr Loftus?

____

2 How does Michael feel about coming back to school?

____

3 What do most of the children bring to school for Miss Mee?

____

4 What did Laura get for Christmas?

____

5 What had the twins looked after over the holidays?

____

6 What are the names of the twins?

____

7 What does Brenda bring into school?

____

8 Put a circle around the words which you think best describe Miss Mee's classroom that morning.

busy happy noisy
miserable cheerful quiet

3 Jeremy the jerbil

After lunch everyone had work to do. Some people were cutting the fronts off Christmas cards and making sets of Number Snap cards. Other people were using the backs of the Christmas cards to make shopping lists for their Mums.

Miss Mee was listening to Asif who was reading to her. Pete and Sue were cleaning out Jeremy's cage, while Wendy sat on the floor and held Jeremy on her lap. The classroom was quite quiet, because everyone was busy.

Suddenly – "SNAP!" shouted Jean and Michael together. Everyone jumped – even Wendy. She let go of Jeremy and he shot off her lap and streaked under the cupboard.

For a moment there was silence, then Pete and Sue shouted:

"Jeremy's gone! He's under the cupboard!"

All the others leapt to their feet, spraying Christmas cards and Snap cards all over the floor. Wendy burst into tears.

"*Sit down*!" said Miss Mee. Everyone sat down.

"And *be quiet*!" said Miss Mee. "We don't want to frighten him."

She tiptoed over to one side of the cupboard; Jeremy's little grey nose and twitchy whiskers peeped out at the other side.

From *Allotment Lane School Again* by Margaret Joy

Different settings

1 The shed was near the house. It was dark because it had only one small window, and that was covered with cobwebs. There were some tools in the shed, a spade and a rake and a hoe, and a pile of old sacks. There was something else as well, that not many people knew about. If you stood quite still in the shed, without moving a hand or a foot, you could hear the crackle of straw and perhaps a tiny cry.

The crackle of straw and the cry came from a box standing in a corner. In the box were a mother cat and her three newborn kittens. The cat's name was Minnie and her kittens were named One, Two and Three,

From *The Ten Tales of Shellover* by Ruth Ainsworth

2 Aunt May's kitchen was clean and bright. Everything sparkled in the morning sunshine because Aunt May was always dusting and polishing, sweeping and mopping. There was never a speck of dirt on the floor, a smudge on the window or crumbs on the table.

There was only one thing out of place in the tidy, clean kitchen. It wasn't something you could see but something you could hear. If you stood very still you could hear the 'drip, drip, drip' of the kitchen tap. No matter how many times Aunt May had called the plumber to come and look at it, the tap still dripped and Aunt May was getting very cross.

YEAR 3 TERM 1

UNIT 2

Dialogue

Learning targets

On completion of this unit children should be able to:

1 ➤ recognise how dialogue is presented in stories, e.g. through statements, questions and exclamations

2 ➤ recognise different voices in stories using dramatised readings showing differences between the narrator and different characters used

3 ➤ read, prepare and present play scripts

4 ➤ recognise the key differences between prose and play script, e.g. by looking at dialogue, stage directions, layout of text in prose and play scripts

5 ➤ write simple play scripts based on own reading and oral work.

Before you start

Background knowledge

At Key Stage 1 the children were given the opportunity to recognise and represent spoken words in the form of speech bubbles. As a lead in, revise the work in *Learning Targets – Grammar and Punctuation Key Stage* 1, Section 8 on direct speech.

This unit builds on that earlier work and introduces the children to how direct speech is set out. Specific teaching of the punctuation can however, be found in *Learning Targets: Grammar and Punctuation Key Stage* 2. The emphasis here in Unit 2 is to focus the children's attention on including conversations in their stories and differentiating between narrative and dialogue. Go over the terms 'statement', 'question' and 'order' before you begin the first session. There is also a model to show the children how to turn a narrative into a play.

Resources for Session 1

Copymasters 5a–b *The Phantom Knicker Nicker*, Copymaster 6 Comprehension, pencils.

Resources for Session 2

Copymaster 7 Conversation Piece, pencils, felt-tip pens.

Resources for Session 3

Copymasters 8a–b *Teeth for Charlie*, Copymaster 9 A play.

Links to other units

Learning Targets: Grammar and Punctuation Key Stage 1, Section 8 on direct speech
Learning Targets: Reading and Writing Key Stage 1, Section 3 on plays

Assessment indicators

- Can the children recognise the difference between dialogue and narrative in stories?
- Can they rewrite parts of stories as plays?

Teaching the sessions

Session 1

Introduction 20-25 min

Give each child **Copymasters 5a–b *The Phanton Knicker Nicker*,** to be used as a shared, whole class text. Explain to the children that this is the beginning of a story about a group of children who decide that they are going to solve mysteries if people will pay them. Read through the copymaster with the children and use the following points as a basis for class discussion.

- 'What are the names of the characters in the story?'
- 'How can you tell when the characters are speaking?'
- 'Find something that Alice/Priya/Vas/Toby says.'
- 'Find an example of one of the characters asking a question.'
- 'Find an example of one of the characters making a statement.'
- 'Find an example of one of the characters giving an order.'

Dialogue and narrative 30 min

Put the children into groups of five so that each child can be one of the following characters: Priya, Alice, Vas, Toby, Sergeant Durkin.

Explain to the children that they are going to read what the characters say. Introduce the term 'dialogue'. The children who are going to read what

Alice says should underline the words she speaks; the children who are going to read what Priya says should underline the words *she* speaks and so on. Working with each group in turn, read the narrative and let the children read the dialogue. When a group has run through the extract once, discuss with the children how they might say their various lines (i.e. intonation).

Comprehension

15-20min

As each group finishes, give individuals a photocopy of **Copymaster 6 Comprehension** to work on.

Homework

The children can finish the comprehension for homework.

Session 2

1 2

Introduction

20-25min

Give each child **Copymaster 7 Conversation Piece**, to be used as a shared, whole class text. Although the poem apparently deals with the death of a grandma, children usually see that Blenkinsop is just using this as an excuse and that it hasn't really happened. Read and enjoy the poem with the children without too much analysis, concentrating rather on the question and answer structure that you are going to ask the children to use as a model for their own writing. Spend some time discussing what sort of people the children think Blenkinsop and the teacher are. What impressions have they gained about them through what they say?

If time permits, some of the children might like to volunteer to read the poem aloud in pairs.

Question and answer

30min

Using the poem as a model, the children can work in pairs and write their own 'Question and Answer' poem. They can base it on the pupil/teacher model of the poem or you can give them other scenarios to choose from, e.g:

- shopper and shopkeeper
- parent and child
- brother and sister.

Tell the children to spend some time planning what their conversation is about and to draft it in rough first. You can also point out that it need not be as long as 'Conversation Piece'. You may want to set a limit of ten lines. When the children are satisfied, they can take it in turns to write the lines in two different coloured felt-tip pens.

Summary

15min

The children can read out their conversations to the class.

Session 3

Introduction

20min

Give each child **Copymasters 8a–b *Teeth for Charlie***, to be used as a shared, whole class text. Read through the copymaster with the children and use the following questions as a basis for class discussion.

- 'Who are the characters in the story?'
- 'Why do you think Charlie puts the second postcard in the bin?'
- 'Do you think he should have done that?'
- 'Do you think his Mum will find out? How?'

Explain to the children that you are now going to look at the same story written as a play. Give each child **Copymaster 9 A play**, and go through it with the children. They should look at the story and the play side by side to match up the dialogue and see how the stage directions and scene setting come from the narrative part of the story. Investigate how the play is set out to differentiate between the spoken words, the actions of the characters and the setting of the scene.

Preparing the play

30min

Put the children into groups of five so they can prepare and present the play. As an extension, the children could write an ending where Mum finds the card.

In a subsequent session, the children can use '*Teeth for Charlie*' as a model and rewrite parts of their favourite stories as plays.

The Phantom Knicker Nicker (1)

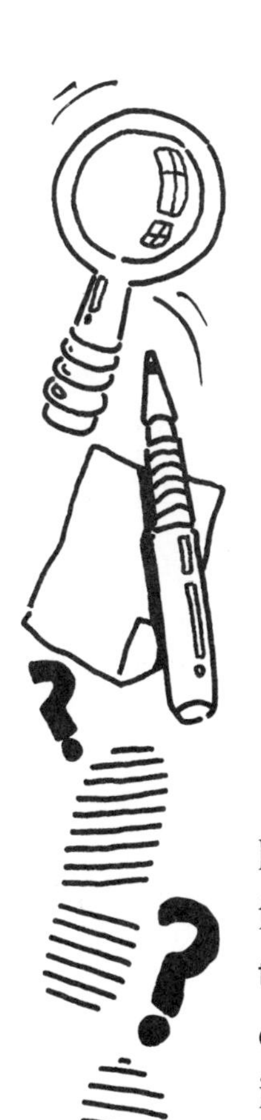

GANG OF FOUR PRIVATE DETECTIVE AGENCY

Priya printed the words carefully in her best handwriting, in bold black felt-tip pen, on the back of an old piece of card. She looked round at the rest of the Gang – little chubby Alice, with her baby blue eyes and cherubic face, long skinny Vas and pink plump Toby. They were seated in a row on top of the wall by the bus shelter on the village green, idly swinging their legs in the summer sunshine.

'What else shall I say?'

Alice took hold of one of the stubby blonde plaits which stuck out like little fat sausages on either side of her head. She did her best to pull it round as far as her mouth. (It was Alice's ambition to be able to chew on the end of it.)

'It was your idea,' said Alice. 'You think what to say.'

'I shall say, **Mysteries Solved**,' said Priya. '**For a Fee**.'

Alice attempted to tie both plaits under her chin in a knot.

'How much are we going to charge?'

'Five pounds?' said Priya.

'Ten,' said Vas. 'Ten if it's dangerous.'

Alice squealed. 'I don't want to do anything dangerous!'

'You might have to,' said Priya. 'When you set out to solve mysteries there's no telling where you might end up.'

Alice put a thumb in her mouth and started to suck.

'What I'll do,' said Priya, picking up the card. 'I'll stick it in the window when my dad's not looking.'

(*Continued*)

The Phantom Knicker Nicker (2)

Priya's dad ran the Tipsy Green post office and newsagent's, just across from the bus shelter where they were sitting. They could see the window quite clearly, with all its cards advertising goods for sale, rooms to let, services for hire. People were supposed to pay 50p a week to have their cards in the window, but the Gang didn't have 50p. They didn't have 20p. They didn't even have 5p. The Gang were broke.

'By this time next week – ' Priya sprang down triumphantly from the wall – 'we'll be rich as rich! And all thanks to me!'

Toby took his specs off and began energetically to polish them. 'That's boasting, that is.'

'Pooh!' said Priya, doing a little showing-off twirl and losing her balance.

Toby hastily put his specs on again as Priya went spinning, out of control, round the corner of the bus shelter. Boing! went Priya, hurtling into someone coming in the opposite direction. A big hand shot out and grabbed her.

'Watch it!' said a familiar voice.

The voice belonged to the Lead Truncheon (otherwise known as Sergeant Durkin of the local nick). The Lead Truncheon was an old enemy.

'What are you lot up to?' he said.

From *The Phantom Knicker Nicker* by Jean Ure

6 Comprehension

1 Whose idea was it to start a detective agency?

Priya

2 What does Alice say that shows she is:

a not very helpful?

It was your idea. You think what to say

b not very brave?

I don't want to do anything dangerous

3 What does Priya say that shows she thinks they are going to get lots of mysteries to solve?

By this time next week we'll be rich as rich

4 What does Sergeant Durkin say that shows you he wants to know what the children are up to?

What are you lot up to?

7 Conversation Piece

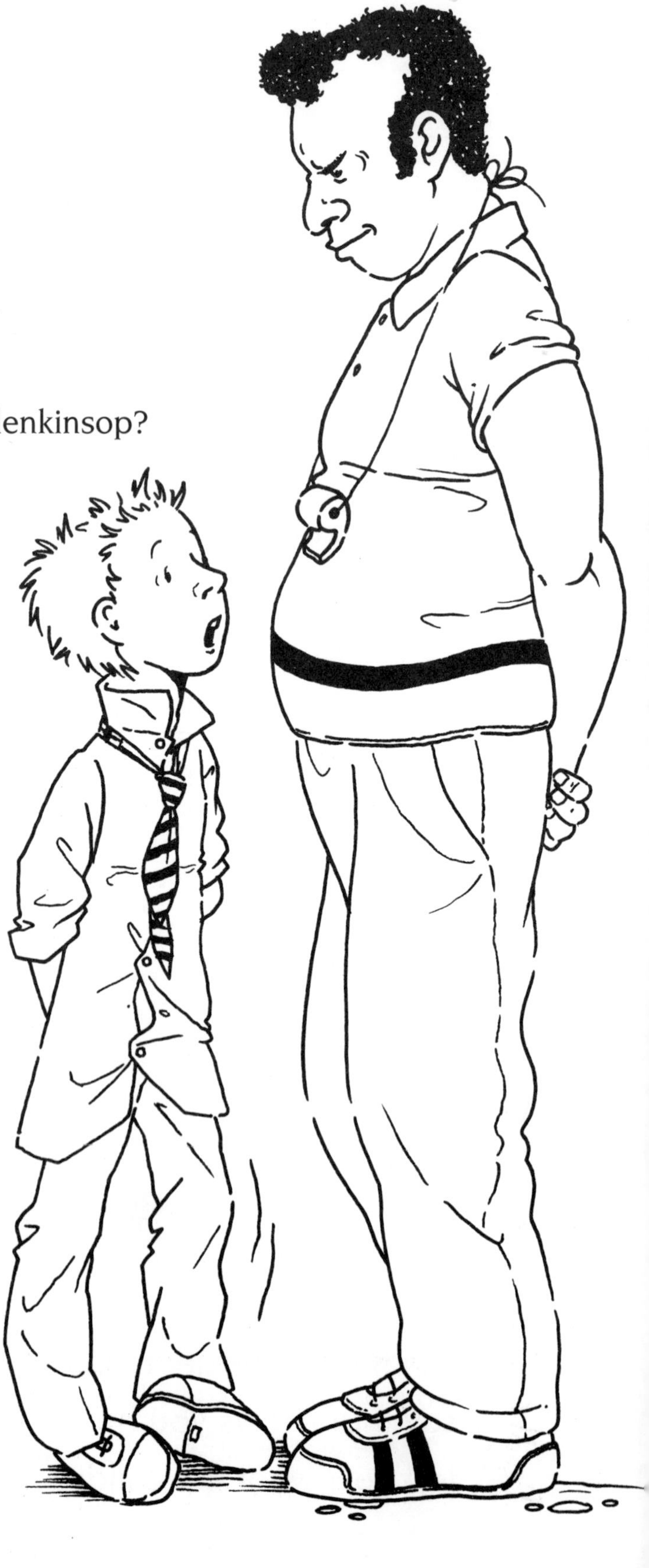

Late again Blenkinsop?
What's the excuse this time?
Not my fault sir.
Whose fault is it then?
Grandma's sir.
Grandma's. What did she do?
She died sir.
Died?
She's seriously dead all right sir.
That makes four grandmothers this term.
And all on P.E. days Blenkinsop.
I know. It's very upsetting sir.
How many grandmothers have you got Blenkinsop?
Grandmothers sir? None.
None?
All dead sir.
And what about yesterday Blenkinsop?
What about yesterday sir?
You missed maths.
That was the dentist sir.
The dentist died?
No sir. My teeth sir.
You missed the test Blenkinsop.
I'd been looking forward to it too sir.
Right, line up for P.E.
Can't sir.
No such word as can't. Why can't you?
No kit sir.
Where is it?
Home sir.
What's it doing at home?
Not ironed sir.
Couldn't you iron it?
Can't do it sir.
Why not?
My hand sir.
Who usually does it?
Grandma sir.
Why couldn't she do it?
Dead sir.

Gareth Owen

Teeth for Charlie (1)

There was a ring at the door-bell.

"See who it is, Charlie!" Mum was busy sewing a button on Mike's football shirt.

Charlie rushed to the door. He almost tripped over Sheeba, the cat. She gave him a cold stare of disapproval.

"It's the postman!" shouted Charlie, as he opened the door.

The postman held out some letters for Charlie.

"Morning, Charlie. Your Aunt Em is at it again!"

"Oh dear! I'll get some money from Mum."

"What is it, Charlie?" Mum joined him at the door.

"Aunt Em has forgotten to put a stamp on her letter again."

"I am sorry! She's getting so absent-minded. It takes her all her time to write a letter, let alone put a stamp on it."

Mum felt in her apron pocket for some money to give the postman.

"There's a postcard from Uncle Tim," Charlie said. "He's coming home from holiday this week. He's coming to see us on Sunday."

There was another card addressed to Mike and Charlie Lavender. Charlie pushed this in his pocket. He felt his face go red.

"There's Josie crying in her pram!" Mum hurried to fetch her in from the garden.

(*Continued*)

Teeth for Charlie (2)

Charlie took the postcard from his pocket and looked at it quickly. It was for an appointment with Mr Parker, the dentist, a week on Friday.

Charlie looked through the kitchen window. He could see Mum talking to Josie as she wheeled her away from the apple tree.

"Just time!" he muttered. He opened the cupboard under the sink and pushed the card into the rubbish bin.

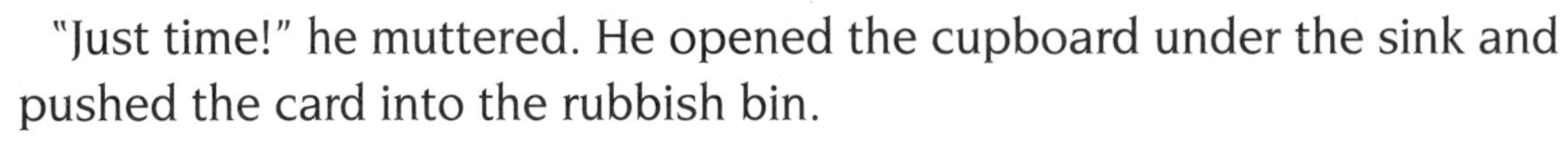

Mum carried Josie into the kitchen. She was still howling. Her eyes were pools of tears which then cascaded down her fat little cheeks.

"Shall I get her a drink?" Charlie asked.

"Thank you, Charlie." Mum sat down and bounced Josie up and down on her knee.

"Let's take your bonnet off" – the ties were sopping wet and difficult to undo.

As Charlie handed her a mug of orange, Josie stopped howling and gave him a watery smile. She made loud sucking noises and the liquid ran down her chin. Mum grabbed a duster, to stop the orange soaking her coat.

The duster smelled of polish. Josie sneezed and wrinkled her nose.

"Pooh! Pooh!" she cried.

Mike came into the kitchen. On Saturday morning he went to Junior Film Club. "It was a super film!" he said. "The Indians captured this girl and the cowboy saved her."

From *Teeth for Charlie* by Joy Allen

A play

[Mum and Charlie are sitting in the kitchen. Mum is sewing a button on Mike's football shirt. The door-bell rings.]

Mum: See who it is, Charlie!

[Charlie rushes to the door and trips over the cat.]

Charlie: *[Charlie opens the door.]* It's the postman!

Postman: *[handing letters to Charlie]* Morning, Charlie. Your Aunt Em is at it again.

Charlie: Oh dear! I'll get some money from Mum.

Mum: *[coming to the door]* What is it, Charlie?

Charlie: Aunt Em has forgotten to put a stamp on her letter again.

Mum: I am sorry! She's getting so absent-minded. It takes her all her time to write a letter, let alone put a stamp on it.

[Mum finds some money in her apron pocket and gives it to the postman]

Charlie: There's a postcard from Uncle Tim. He's coming home from holiday this week. He's coming to see us on Sunday.

[Charlie looks at another postcard, he goes red and pushes it into his pocket]

Mum: There's Josie crying in her pram.

[Mum hurries out of the room. Charlie looks at the postcard again which is a dental appointment on Friday. He looks through the kitchen window to see what his Mum is doing.]

Charlie: Just time!

[Charlie pushes the postcard into the rubbish bin, Mum returns with Josie who is crying]

Charlie: Shall I get her a drink?

Mum: Thank you Charlie. *[sitting down and talking to Josie]* Let's take your bonnet off.

[Charlie gives Josie a mug of orange and she spills some down her chin. Mum wipes it up with a duster.]

Josie: Pooh! Pooh!

[Mike enters the kitchen. He has been to the Junior Film Club.]

Mike: It was a super film! The Indians captured a girl and a cowboy saved her!

YEAR 3 TERM 1

UNIT 3

Poetry writing

Learning targets

On completion of this unit children should be able to:

1 ➤ read aloud and recite poems, comparing different views of the same subject, discussing choice of words and phrases that describe and create impact

2 ➤ distinguish between rhyming and non-rhyming poetry and comment on the impact of the layout

3 ➤ invent a range of shape poems, selecting appropriate words and presenting them carefully.

Before you start

Background knowledge

Learning Targets: Reading and Writing Key Stage 1 introduced the children to the concept of rhyme, nursery rhymes, poems with recognisable patterns, limericks, acrostics, narrative and descriptive poetry. If the children have not experienced these areas of poetry, it is a good idea to do some of this basic work first, before beginning to attempt the following sessions.

This unit introduces the children to the impact of language and layout of poetry using rhyming and non-rhyming poems based on observation.

Resources for Session 1

Copymaster 10 Cats, pencils, paper.

Resources for Session 2

Copymaster 11 Shape poems, pencils, paper.

Links to other units

Learning Targets: Reading and Writing Key Stage 1, Section 1 on poetry

Assessment indicators

- Can the children distinguish between rhyming and non-rhyming poetry?
- Can they pick out and discuss words and phrases in poetry which create impact?
- Can they comment on the layout of a poem?
- Can they create their own shape poems?

Teaching the sessions

Session 1 ①

Introduction — 20 min

Give each child **Copymaster 10 Cats** to be used as a shared, whole class text. Read through the poems with the children and use the following points as a basis for class discussion, paying particular attention to the poets' choice of vocabulary.

'Cats' by Francis Scarfe
the rhyming words
the words (adjectives) used to describe the cats
why the poet says they have 'eyes of gold'
why the people stop to stroke the cats

'Cat in the Dark' by John Agard
the rhyming words
the descriptions – 'a flash of fur', 'gone like a ghost', 'two tiny green traffic lights'

Compare the two poems. Consider the layout – 'Cats' has long lines reflecting the slow-moving, old cats while 'Cat in the Dark' has short lines reflecting the speed at which the cat moves. Which poem do the children prefer? Why?

Contrast — 20 min

Give each small group a contrasting pair of animals to consider, e.g:

- an old dog/a puppy
- an elephant/a horse
- a tortoise/a rabbit.

Explain to the children that you want them to discuss what their pair of animals look like and how they move. One member of the group can compile a list of words and phrases that they have agreed would describe their animals.

Summary — 10 min

Each group can report back to the class on their word lists. Use this opportunity to expand the children's vocabulary. If a group has used the word 'big' to describe an elephant, ask the class whether they can think of more interesting words, such as 'enormous', 'gigantic' or 'huge'.

My own poem 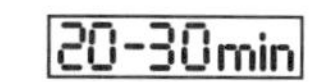

Ask the children to choose one of their animals and write a poem about it, concentrating on what it looks like and how it moves. Remind the children that it does not have to rhyme to be a poem and be on hand to help with 'editing' as the children work.

Homework

Poems can be finished and illustrated at home.

Session 2

2 3

Introduction 10min

Give each child **Copymaster 11 Shape poems**, to be used as a whole class, shared text. Read through the poems and discuss them concentrating on how they look different from 'normal' poems; why they are the shape they are; how the words have been laid out to form the shape; whether they rhyme or not.

My own shape poem 15min

Ask the children to write a shape poem of their own. Some children will have little difficulty with this, whereas others will need help and support in choosing a suitable 'object' to shape their poem on. It sometimes helps to get the children to draw the object in pencil first and then write words which describe what the object looks like over the pencil lines. The poems can be coloured and displayed.

10 Cats

Cats

Those who love cats which do not even purr,
Or which are thin and tired and very old,
Bend down to them in the street and stroke their fur
And rub their ears and smooth their breast, and hold
Their paws, and gaze into their eyes of gold.

Francis Scarfe

Cat in the Dark

Look at that!
Look at that!

But when you look
there's no cat.

Without a purr
just a flash of fur
and gone
like a ghost.

The most
you see
are two tiny
green traffic lights
staring into the night.

John Agard

11 Shape poems

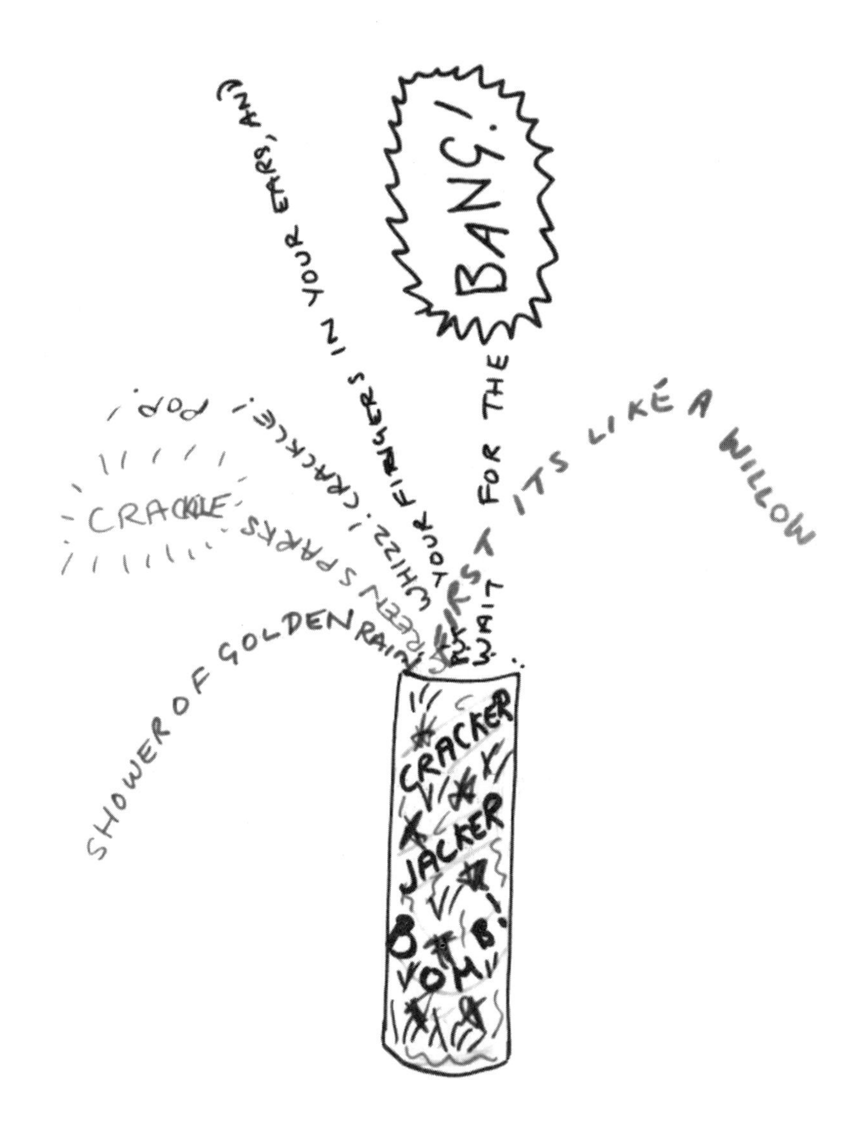

THE CAT
IS SLY A CREEPY
ANIMAL, POUNCING
SLEEPING, WASHING
DAILY IT IS A
MULTI COLOURED
ANIMAL CAN
BE
BLACK, WHITE
SLEEP AT DAY
OR NIGHT BUT FRO
BEST OF ALL IT AND
LOVES A FIGHT TO
IT'S ALL RIGHT TO SWAYING
BE A CAT BUT ONE
YOU MUST EN - WAVING
COUNTER BEING A
A KITTEN. THE IS
CAT'S PAWS TAIL
ARE VELVET ITS
SOFT AS CATS AND
PAWS ALWAYS ARE

12 Stories with familiar settings

Ben was thirsty. That's what must have woken him up. He climbed out of bed and made his way down the stairs to the kitchen,

The house was very dark and quiet. The moon, shining through the hall window, cast strange shadows about the place. As he passed his Dad's bedroom door he could hear him snoring. The stairs creaked under his feet. He had never noticed it in the daytime but the noise seemed very loud at night. He made his way through the hall to the kitchen.

In the kitchen Ben felt his way along the wall until he came to the cupboard where Mum kept the cups. He opened the door which squeaked loudly and made him jump. He took a cup and felt his way over to the sink. He turned on the tap and the water came out with a whoosh, wetting the front of his pyjamas.

Suddenly he could hear noises upstairs. A bed creaked and there was the sound of footsteps on the landing. He would be in real trouble if he was caught downstairs.

1 Where was Ben at the beginning of the story? ____________________

2 Which way did Ben go to get to the kitchen? ____________________

____

3 Make a list of the noises Ben could hear as he made his way to the kitchen. ____________________

____

4 Make a list of the noises Ben heard while he was in the kitchen.

____

5 How do you think Ben was feeling as he made his way to the kitchen? ____________________

____

13 Plays

Rewrite the passage below as a play.

Totty was staying with his grandfather and one day he showed Totty a book with pictures of wild animals.

Almost at the end of the book there was a picture of two dark grey creatures lolling in the shallow water of some strange river. They had heavy heads and tiny eyes and huge, bristling upper lips. Their forelegs looked rather like canoe-paddles, and Totty couldn't see any back legs at all.

'They're fish,' said Totty.

'No,' said his grandfather, 'They're not fish. They're animals called Manatees. It says so here.'

Totty stared at the Manatees in the picture, and thought. Then he asked, 'What do Manatees eat?'

But either his grandfather did not want to answer that question, or he did not hear it – he was an old man, and rather deaf. He shut the animal book with a snap and said, 'Time for bed, young Totty!'

From *Lion at School and Other Stories* by Phillipa Pearce

Poetry

Read the poem and answer the questions.

I Meant to Do My Work Today

I meant to do my work today –
But a brown bird sang in the apple tree,
And a butterfly flitted across the field,
And the leaves were calling to me.

And the wind went sighing over the land
Tossing the grasses to and fro,
And a rainbow held out its shining hand –
So what could I do but laugh and go?

Richard le Gallienne

1 The poet does not do his work because he sees and hears things which make him want to go outside.

a What does the poet see? ______________________________

____

____

b What does the poet hear? ______________________________

____

____

2 When the poet says 'the leaves were calling to me', what do you think they might have been saying? ______________________________

____

____

3 If you were the poet would you have done your work or gone outside? Why? ______________________________

____

____

YEAR 3 TERM 2

Focus

In this section children will be given the opportunity to look at a variety of traditional stories concentrating on typical themes and characters. They can use the extracts as models to create story plans and characters.

Content

Unit 1: Traditional stories
Unit 2: Characters
Unit 3: Story plans

Reading List

'Phaethon' from *Of Gods and Goddessess*, Ginn Reading 360, 1979

Nutt, David *Celtic Fairy Tales*, Studio Edition, 1994

Ridgway, Bill *Lo Shi and the Word-seller*, Arnold-Wheaton, 1986

Wade, Barrie and Moore, Maggie '*Watch What You Say*', Thomas Nelson and Sons Ltd, Story Chest, 1986

Assessment

Assessment Copymasters 21–22 are at the end of the section.

Copymasters 21a–b *Sir Gawain and the Green Knight*

Reading comprehension: this is a 'potted' version of a traditional story and assesses literal comprehension as well as providing the opportunity to write an ending.

Copymaster 22 Traditional tales

Writing composition: children can plan and write a traditional story from a selection of openings, characters and traditional themes.

National Literacy Strategy planner

This chart shows you how to find activities by unit to resource your term's requirements for text level work on fiction and poetry. The Learning Targets closely follow the structure of the fiction and poetry requirements for the term in the National Literacy Strategy document (pages 34–5). A few of the requirements are not covered. These are usually the ones that require extended reading or writing or comparison of several different texts.

YEAR 3 TERM 2

Range

Fiction and poetry:

- myths
- legends
- parables
- traditional stories
- stories with related themes
- oral and performance poetry from different cultures.

TEXT LEVEL WORK

COMPREHENSION AND COMPOSITION

Reading comprehension

Pupils should be taught:

1 to investigate the styles and voices of traditional story language – collect examples, e.g. story openings and endings; scene openers, e.g. '*Now when* …', 'A *long time ago* …'; list, compare and use in own writing: Unit 1;

2 to identify typical story themes, e.g. trials and forfeits, good over evil, weak over strong, wise over foolish: Units 1 and 3;

3 to identify and discuss main and recurring characters, evaluate their behaviour and justify views: Units 2 and 3;

4 to choose and prepare poems for performance, identifying appropriate expression, tone, volume and use of voices and other sounds: Section 1, Units 2 and 3;

5 rehearse and improve performance, taking note of punctuation and meaning;

Writing composition

Pupils should be taught:

6 to plan main points of a structure for story writing, considering how to capture points in a few words that can be elaborated later; discuss different methods of planning: Units 2 and 3;

7 to describe and sequence key incidents in a variety of ways, e.g. by listing, charting, mapping, making simple storyboards: Unit 2;

8 to write portraits of characters, using story text to describe behaviour and characteristics, and presenting portraits in a variety of ways, e.g. as posters, labelled diagrams, letters to friends about them: Unit 2;

9 to write a story plan for own myth, fable or traditional tale, using story theme from reading but substituting different chacters or changing the setting: Unit 3;

10 to write alternative sequels to traditional stories using same characters and settings, identifying typical phrases and expressions from stories and using these to help structure the writing: Unit 2;

11 to write new or extended verses for performance based on models of 'performance' and oral poetry read, e.g. rhythms, repetition: Section 1 Units 2 and 3.

YEAR 3 TERM 2

UNIT 1

Traditional stories

Learning targets

On completion of this unit children should be able to:

1 ➤ investigate the styles and voices of traditional story language, story and scene openers

2 ➤ identify some typical story themes

3 ➤ write own traditional story openings.

Before you start

Background knowledge

This unit introduces the children to some typical elements in traditional stories. Before beginning Session 1, have a general class discussion to ascertain the children's depth of knowledge. Have they heard of the terms 'myth' and 'legend'? Do they consider fairy stories to be 'traditional tales'? At this stage, it is not necessary to draw fine distinctions between the above terms. Rather, it is the emphasis of the unit to establish typical themes that these stories often deal with and to look at how to begin a traditional tale.

Resources for Session 1

Copymaster 15 Story openings, Copymaster 16 Opening sentences, pencils, paper.

Links to other units

Learning Targets: Reading and Writing Key Stage 1, Section 2 Unit 4 on fairy stories

Assessment indicators

- Can the children identify and discuss elements of traditional tales?
- Can they write the opening to a traditional tale?

Teaching the sessions

Session 1 ① ② ③

Introduction 30 min

Begin the session by asking the children what they understand by a 'traditional tale'. They may not have come across this term before but some of the children may respond by saying 'fairy stories'. Through class discussion, introduce the terms 'myth' and 'legend' and try to arrive at a point where the children grasp the fact that traditional tales were usually written a long time ago.

Give each child **Copymaster 15 Story openings**, to be used as a whole class, shared text. Explain that you are going to look at the openings of three traditional tales and see if you can find out some of the things traditional tales were written about. Read through the copymaster with the children and base a class discussion on the following points:

Lo Shi and the Word-seller

- 'When does the story take place?' (long ago)
- 'Where does the story take place?' (China)
- 'Who is the main character?' (Lo Shi)
- 'What does he do for a living?' (merchant)
- 'What is he going to do at the beginning of the story?' (go on a journey)

Hudden and Dudden and Donald O'Neary

- 'When do the children think that the story took place?' (long ago, i.e. 'once upon a time')
- 'Would they describe Hudden and Dudden as rich or poor?' (rich)
- 'Would they describe Donald as rich or poor?' (poor)
- 'How did Hudden and Dudden feel about Donald?' (jealous of him, not helpful or friendly towards him)
- 'What did Donald have that Hudden and Dudden wanted?' (a poor strip of land)
- 'Why do you think they wanted it?' ('the more one has, the more one wants')

Phaethon

- 'What tells you this story was written a long time ago? (gods/the sun travelling across the sky)
- 'How did the Greeks explain that the sun seemed to move across the sky? (they thought the sun was Apollo's fiery chariot)
- 'Do we think the sun moves? (Hopefully 'no'! The Earth moves around the sun.)

Tell the children that many traditional tales deal with the same sorts of things that they have been discussing and try to reach a conclusion. Recurring themes deal with the issues listed overleaf.

- Characters who go on long journeys to make their fortune.
- Characters who are opposites, e.g. rich and poor; good and evil; wise and foolish, where the poor/good/wise characters usually win in the end.
- Gods and goddesses believed in by ancient people.
- Stories to explain things that the people of the time could not explain scientifically, e.g. the sun rising and setting.
- Most countries have their own traditional tales.

Write the list of themes on the board.

Stress that traditional tales are about people and events from long ago. Our fairy stories are a form of traditional tales, as are the legends about King Arthur.

Opening sentences

Give each group a photocopy of **Copymaster 16 Opening sentences**. Choose one child from each group to fill in the copymaster after group discussion.

Explain to the children that they are going to write the opening sentence (s) for these four traditional tales and they must keep in mind the things they have been discussing. It is usually quite helpful to give examples of the things they should not write. Ask the children if they could have a supermarket/ aeroplane/computer in the their opening sentence(s)?

Go around as the children are working to see whether their discussions are along the right lines and 'lead' them if necessary.

'Once upon a time…' This sentence is open ended so the story could be about almost anything. You could ask who the main character is going to be and try to get the children to write about a character who appears to have nothing going for him/her at the start of the story. Encourage the children to draw on their knowledge of fairy stories.

'In China there once lived two families who…' Remind the children of the characters in 'Hudden and Dudden and Donald O'Neary' to point them towards having the two families in very different circumstances, e.g. one rich, one poor; one kind, one selfish and greedy, etc.

'Zeus, the king of the gods was angry and…' Ask the children who he might have been angry with, e.g. another god/humans. What did he do when he was angry? How might the people on Earth know that Zeus was angry?'

'Once a poor shepherd set out on a long journey to …' Where was the shepherd going? Why do many characters in traditional tales go on long journeys?

Summary

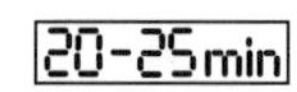

Ask each group in turn to read out the opening sentence(s) of the traditional tale that begins 'Once upon a time'. Through discussion, find out whether the children think it is a good opening. Does it 'sound' like a traditional tale? Is there anything in it which is similar to the openings they have read and discussed?

Do this for each story opening. If the children include other traditional story elements like magic, witches, heroes, etc. add these to the list of themes on the board.

Story openings

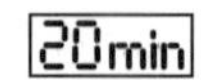

Explain to the children that they are going to write an opening for their own traditional tale. Go over the kinds of things they could write about and refer them to the list of themes on the board. Remind them that their story could take place anywhere in the world so long as it is set long ago. They should attempt at least three or four sentences.

Homework

The children can finish their story openings at home and illustrate them. Add them to the book display in the classroom around the theme of traditional tales.

15 Story openings

Lo Shi and the Word-seller

Long ago in China there lived a merchant by the name of Lo Shi. One day he said to his wife, "I am joining a party of merchants. Tomorrow we are going to the distant town by the Great Wall, where we have heard that trade is good. It may be some time before I see you again.'

Hudden and Dudden and Donald O'Neary

There was once upon a time two farmers, and their names were Hudden and Dudden. They had poultry in their yards, sheep on the uplands, and scores of cattle in the meadow-land alongside the river. But for all that they weren't happy. For just between their two farms there lived a poor man by the name of Donald O'Neary. He had a hovel over his head and a strip of grass that was barely enough to keep his one cow, Daisy, from starving, and, though she did her best, it was but seldom that Donald got a drink of milk or a roll of butter from Daisy. You would think there was little here to make Hudden and Dudden jealous, but so it is, the more one has the more one wants, and Donald's neighbours lay awake of nights scheming how they might get hold of his little strip of grass-land.

Phaethon

The Greeks believed that their gods dwelt on the top of a high mountain called Olympus. Among them was Phoebus Apollo, god of music and medicine as well as god of the sun. It was he who drove the fiery chariot, drawn by four winged horses, across the sky each day. Every morning, heading out from the Gates of Dawn, Phoebus drove his chariot up into the sky and straight across the heavens, until at last he reached the spot where his course descended into the western ocean and Night arrived.

16 Opening sentences

Once upon a time ______________________________

In China there once lived two families who ______________________________

Zeus, the king of the gods was angry and ______________________________

Once a poor shepherd set out on a long journey to ______________________________

YEAR 3 TERM 2

UNIT **2**

Characters

Learning targets

On completion of this unit children should be able to:

1 ➤ identify and discuss characters; evaluate behaviour and justify views

2 ➤ describe and sequence key incidents in a variety of ways, e.g. by listing, charting, mapping and making simple storyboards

3 ➤ write portraits of characters, using story text to describe behaviour and characteristics – present portraits in a variety of ways: posters, labelled diagrams, letters to friends

4 ➤ write alternative sequels/endings to traditional stories using the same characters and settings.

Before you start

Background knowledge

The work in this unit is based on the traditional Spanish folk tale '*Watch What You Say*'. The story is used to explore story structure/plot, look at the behaviour of the characters and provide an opportunity for children to write alternative endings or sequels.

The structure of these sessions can be applied to any traditional story that you might be using with your class.

Resources for Session 1

Copymasters 17a–d *Watch What You Say* large sheets of paper, A4 paper, glue, pencils, felt-tip pens.

Resources for Session 2

Copymasters 17a–d *Watch What You Say*, large sheets of paper, felt-tip pens.

Resources for Session 3

Pencils, paper.

Links to other units

Learning Targets: Reading and Writing Key Stage 1, Section 2 Unit 1 on plot, Unit 2 on character and Unit 7 on traditional stories

Assessment indicators

- Can the children recognise key incidents in a story?
- Can they describe character and evaluate behaviour?
- Given certain limitations, can they add episodes to a story?

Teaching the sessions

Session 1 ❷

Introduction 30–40min

Give each child **Copymasters 17a–d *Watch What You Say***. Staple the sheets together before you give them out. Read through the story with the children.

Through class discussion, sequence the key events. It is important that the children appreciate that Rohan is playing a linguistic trick: he is taking literally the things that his mother is saying instead of recognising what she actually means. Look through the story again and ask the children to help you make a list on the board of the jobs Rohan's mother wanted him to do, what she actually said and what she actually meant.

The job	What she said	What she meant
fetching water	'Now jump to it.'	get a move on/ do it now
do the housework	'turn over a new leaf'	start behaving differently/better
close the door	'pull the front door after you'	not to leave the door open when you leave the house

Can the children explain how Rohan's mother got her own back? She played the same trick on him by taking what he said literally.

What Rohan asked his mother to do	What he said	What he meant
not to make him eat any more	'Please leave me alone'	to stop forcing food on him and let him sleep.

Can the children think of any more examples? E.g.:

- Pull up your socks. (do better)
- Put your shoulder to the wheel. (try harder)
- Put your cards on the table. (tell the truth)

Mapping the plot 20-30min

In groups the children can detail the plot of the story *Watch What You Say*. At this stage the work should be done in draft form.

Summary 10-15 min

Let each group share their work with the class.

- 'Can anyone spot anything which has been left out?'
- 'Are any of the events in the wrong order?'
- 'Has any group included details which are not "plot" but should be categorised as "character" or "setting"?'

A final draft for display 20min

Ask the children to use their first draft (with corrections, deletions and additions) as the basis for a final draft for display. They can present it in one of the following ways:

- as a flow diagram
- as a simple storyboard.

As sequencing events naturally falls into sections, help the children in each group to share out the work. They must include text and illustration in each section of the plot. The final plot sequence will be glued to large sheets of paper for display.

Homework

Each child can complete their section of the plot sequence ready to stick onto a large sheet of paper for display.

Session 2

Introduction 20min

Begin by giving each child Copymasters 17a–d *Watch What You Say* and revise the story. Explain that you are now going to concentrate on the characters. Base a whole class discussion on the following questions:

- 'Who are the main characters in the story?'
- 'Are there any characters who do not say anything?'

The main characters

Consider Rohan and his mother as the two main characters. Ask the children to help you compile a list of words and phrases to describe their impressions of them. What do they think of the way Rohan behaved? What do they think of the way his mother behaved?

The non-speaking characters

The children should have identified Gozo and the villagers as characters who did not say anything. Can the children say why these characters are included in the story?

Making character portraits 20-30min

In groups, the children can discuss and identify the characteristics of the two main characters. They should find evidence from the story to support their views. At this stage, the work should be done in draft form.

Summary 10-15 min

Let each group share their work with the class. Can anyone spot anything that has been left out? Has any group included details which are not 'character' but should be categorised as 'plot' or 'setting'?

A final draft for display 20-30min

Explain to the children that they are now going to use their first draft (with corrections, deletions and additions) as the basis for a final draft for display. They can present it as either a 'wanted' poster or as a labelled diagram.

Help the children in each group to share out the work. They must include text and illustration so some of the children could be responsible for the drawing/colouring while others could make labels or headings by hand or using a word processor. The final poster or diagram will be glued to large sheets of paper for display.

Homework

Ask the children to imagine that they are either Rohan or his mother. Write a letter to the aunt on the island of Gozo complaining about the behaviour of the other character.

Session 3 ④

Introduction 10min

Explain to the children that they are now going to consider 'what would have happened next' if:

- Rohan had really learned his lesson
- he went back to his old ways.

Writing the next episode 30min

The children must plan and write the next episode of the story using one of the above scenarios.

Homework

The children can finish writing and illustrating their episodes.

Watch What You Say (1)

Rohan and his mother lived in a stone cottage in a fishing village not far from Valetta in Malta. Rohan was really a very lazy boy. His mother worked hard to make life good for them, but Rohan did not help unless she forced him to.

When the sun shone Rohan became dreamy and went to sit in the shade. While other boys went to fish for mullet or sardines, Rohan stayed at home. He lay on his bed or perhaps he would play with his pet lizard, Gozo. Rohan had found the lizard sunbathing on a rock when they went to visit his aunt on the island of Gozo. He could not be bothered to think of a better name to call a lizard, so he called it Gozo.

"You are a fine pair, you and that lizard," his mother said angrily one morning. "All you do is lie about the house doing nothing. I have had enough. Here, take this bucket. Go to the well and fetch water for us. Come, now jump to it."

Rohan took the bucket and slowly walked into the street. Then, like a frog, he began to jump, swinging the bucket in his hand until he reached the well. When he had filled the bucket with water, he began to jump again, both feet together. He jumped all the way home and, of course, the water splashed out of the bucket as he went.

When he reached his cottage, there was no water left.

His mother said, "Where is the water I wanted?"

"It splashed out when I jumped," Rohan answered.

"You stupid boy," his mother shouted. "Why didn't you walk carefully?"

"Because you told me to jump to it," said Rohan.

After that his mother fetched the water herself, but Rohan's laziness still made her angry.

One day, when Rohan and Gozo were both lying outside stretched in the early summer sunshine, she grew very, very cross.

"You good-for-nothing, lazy boy," she cried. "I have had enough. Now you can do all the work in the house for me, while I go to the market. You never help me at all. This time you must turn over a new leaf."

Rohan went into the kitchen sulkily and his mother walked off to the market.

When she came back, there was no fire lit for cooking. The dirty pots and pans were still dirty. The floor had not been swept. There was no sign of Rohan or of Gozo.

Watch What You Say (2)

Angrily she began to do her housework but, when it was finished, there was still no sign of them.

As the sun began to sink behind the cottage roof, she went to look for them. In the field nearby was an olive tree. Under its leafy shade was Rohan with Gozo on the ground beside him. Both had their eyes closed. It looked as if they had been asleep for some time.

"Wake up, you ungrateful boy," she cried. "I have been working all day, while you have been asleep again."

Gozo's eyes flew open, but Rohan only stretched himself.

"What's the matter, mother?" he yawned. "I did what you said."

"What do you mean?" his mother cried.

"Well, you told me to turn over a new leaf, so I found the first tree I could. After I'd turned one of its leaves over, I must have gone to sleep. I expect you are really pleased with me."

His mother was so angry she could hardly speak. She decided she was never going to be tricked again.

The next day, she made Rohan get out of bed before she went to market.

"Now," she said, "I will carry my basket to market when it is empty and you will carry it back when it is full."

"Yes, mother," said Rohan.

He took so long to eat his breakfast that his mother said,

"I must go or I will miss the best bargains. You will have to come to meet me. Don't forget to pull the front door after you."

"Yes, mother, I will do as you say," said Rohan.

His mother went to market and bought their food. She waited and waited, but Rohan did not come. At last she began to walk back home.

As she walked up the village street, she saw a very strange sight. There was Rohan with the door of their cottage tied to a piece of rope. He was pulling it behind him and a crowd of people were following and laughing.

"What on earth are you doing. Rohan?" she cried, when he reached her.

"Why, mother," said Rohan, "I am doing what you told me to do. When you left, you said I had to pull the door after me and that is what I am doing."

Watch What You Say (3)

His mother was so angry that she could not talk. She was tired with carrying the heavy basket and now there were her friends and neighbours laughing at the ridiculous sight. However, she was wise and did not make a fuss in the street.

"Well, let's take the door back home," she said.

Rohan pulled the door back and fixed it in place. Then he went to lie in the sunshine with Gozo, while his mother worked to make their food.

She made a very large meal and Rohan ate two helpings.

"Come on, Rohan, eat some more," she said.

"All right," Rohan said, and he had a third plateful.

"Have some more," his mother said. Rohan was now very sleepy, but he forced himself to eat a fourth helping. Then he stretched himself out on the bed to sleep.

"Have some more to eat," his mother urged him. "Don't leave any."

"I can't eat any more," said Rohan. His eyes were closing and he felt drowsy.

"But there's only a little left," his mother said.

"Oh please let me sleep," Rohan said. "I can't eat any more."

"Just a spoonful," his mother said.

"Oh, mother, I can't. Please leave me alone." Then Rohan's eyes closed and he fell fast asleep.

He slept all that evening and all night. When he woke the next day, he stayed in bed until he felt really hungry. He knew it must be dinner time.

"Mother," he called, and then again. "Mother!"

There was no answer and there was no smell of cooking.

Rohan found Gozo and took him into bed. The lizard's eyes were half closed.

"She's gone to market, I expect," Rohan said. "We'll wait for her."

Rohan waited all that day, but by the evening she still had not come. He could find not a scrap of food in the house. Rohan spent a hungry, uncomfortable night.

Next morning she still had not come back. Rohan dressed and went to talk to the neighbours, but no one knew where his mother was.

Rohan was so thirsty. He had to take the bucket to the well to get water. Later that day he went with his mother's basket to market for

Watch What You Say (4)

food, but he had very little money and could only buy a cabbage. He ate that raw and drank some water. The next day he had nothing to eat. All night his empty stomach grumbled and growled.

The next day he went to the harbour, looking for food. A boy was fishing.

"Please teach me how to fish," said Rohan. "I am so very hungry."

The boy lent Rohan a rod and line and showed him what to do. Rohan fished all day, but he caught nothing. All he had that night was a drink of water. To take his mind off the hunger pains in his stomach, he picked up the broom and swept all the floors of the cottage.

Next morning he went back to the harbour wall. He fished all day. This time he was lucky. He caught two small brill. He took them home and made a fire to cook them. It was easy to put them in the pan, because they were flat fish. The smell was delicious.

Just as they were cooked, the door opened and in came his mother.

"Well," she said, "this is nice – my favourite food!" She helped herself to one of the brill and began to eat it with great pleasure.

"What a lovely, tidy house this is," she said. "You have been busy."

"But where have you been? I could have starved," cried Rohan.

"Oh, I am sorry to hear that," his mother said. "Don't you remember the last thing you said to me? 'Leave me alone,' you said, so I did. I went to visit my sister on Gozo."

Rohan looked at his mother and her eyes were twinkling. He saw how she understood about his lazy ways and how he could never use the same trick again.

From *Watch What You Say* by Ann Wade and Maggie Moore

YEAR 3 TERM 2

UNIT 3

Story plans

Learning targets

On completion of this unit children should be able to:

1 ➼ investigate the styles and voices of traditional story language

2 ➼ write a story plan for own myth or traditional tale using story themes from reading but substituting different characters or changing the setting.

Before you start

Background knowledge

This unit gives the children the opportunity to explore another style of traditional tale: those which teach a lesson or have a moral. These sessions cover fables and parables, as well as looking at how these sorts of traditional tales were often expressed in verse.

Examples of fables and parables are given on the copymasters but, as you may wish the children to research others from the Bible or books of Aesop's fables, have simple versions of these texts available in the classroom.

Resources for Session 1

Copymaster 18 Fables and parables, pencils, felt-tip pens, paper.

Resources for Session 2

Copymaster 19 The Blind Men and the Elephant, Copymaster 20 What did they think it was?

Links to other units

Learning Targets: Reading and Writing Key Stage 1 Section 1 Unit 5 on narrative poetry and Section 2 Unit 4 on fairy stories

Assessment indicators

- Can the children recognise a traditional tale which teaches a lesson?
- Can they plan and write a traditional tale which teaches a lesson?

Teaching the sessions

Session 1 ➀ ➁

Introduction 20-30min

Recap on what the children have learned about traditional stories in terms of language and recurring themes. Explain that there are many traditional tales from many different cultures which have something else in common, i.e. they teach a lesson.

Give each child **Copymaster 18 Fables and parables**. Explain the dictionary definition of the two terms.

fable a tale, especially with animals, conveying a moral

parable a story with imagined events to illustrate a moral or spiritual lesson

Read through the fable and the parable with the children, discussing each in turn to bring out the following points:

- the main characters
- their behaviour
- the 'lesson' each story is teaching
- any similarities or differences between the two stories.

Do the children know of any other stories which teach a lesson? They may be familiar with other parables from the Bible but, although they may know such stories as 'The Tortoise and the Hare' and 'The Mouse and the Lion', they may not recognise them as fables. Recount these two stories to the children and discuss the lesson each one teaches.

'The Tortoise and the Hare'

Hare challenges Tortoise to a race which it seems obvious he will win. Tortoise accepts the challenge and they both set off. After a while, Hare is so far in front that he stops for a rest and falls asleep. While his is sleeping, Tortoise keeps plodding on and wins the race.
Lesson:

- More haste, less speed.
- Overconfidence is not always wise.
- Keep trying and you will succeed.

'The Mouse and the Lion'

A mouse ran over the sleeping body of a lion. The lion woke up and seized the mouse. He was just about to eat it when the mouse said that if he was spared he would repay the lion's kindness. The lion thought that the idea of the mouse ever being able to help him was so funny, that he let the mouse go. Not long afterwards, the lion was caught in a net by hunters. The mouse came along, gnawed through the net and set the lion free.

Lesson:

- You should be kind to others because you never know when you will need their help.
- Just because someone seems less able than you in one set of circumstances, it does not mean that they can't help you in a different set of circumstances.

How will you teach the lesson? 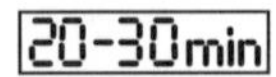

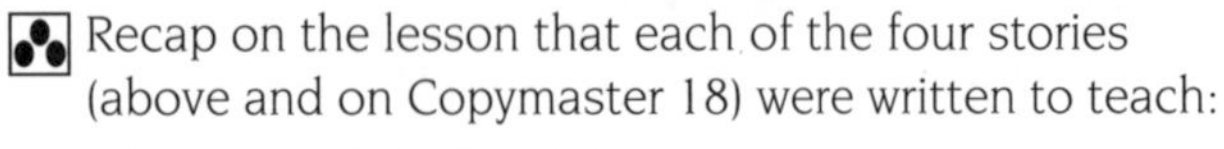

Recap on the lesson that each of the four stories (above and on Copymaster 18) were written to teach:

'The Ant and the Beetle':

- It is not always wise to live just for today.
- Future planning is important.

'The Good Samaritan':

- You should be a 'neighbour' to everyone not just those people you know and like.

'The Tortoise and the Hare':

- Overconfidence is not always wise.

'The Mouse and the Lion':

- Sometimes the weak can help the strong.

Put the children into groups. Ask each group to choose one of the above 'lessons' and make up a different story to illustrate it. The story can be a fable with animal characters, or a parable with human characters.

Summary 

The groups can compare their ideas through class discussion.

Writing the story 20-30min

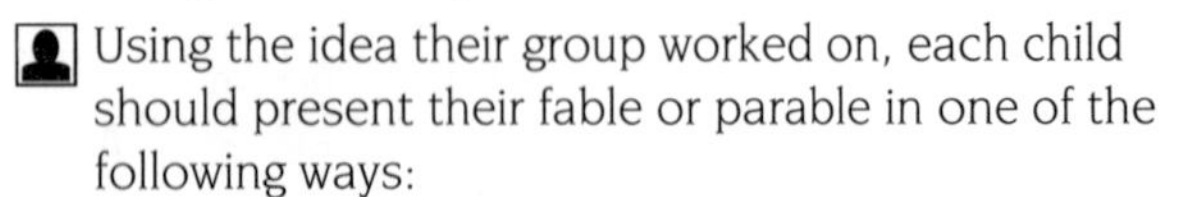

Using the idea their group worked on, each child should present their fable or parable in one of the following ways:

- as a piece of continuous prose
- in a 'comic strip' format with speech bubbles and narrative text
- as a flow diagram detailing the key events.

Homework

The children can complete their story at home.

Session 2 

Introduction 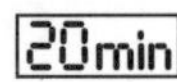

Explain to the children that you are going to look at one more traditional tale which, like those in Session 1, teaches a lesson. It is not, however, written as a story but as a narrative poem. Recap on what the children can remember from their work on narrative poetry in *Learning Targets: Reading and Writing Key Stage 1* where they looked at 'Dad and the Cat and the Tree' and 'On Monday Morning'. Hopefully they will remember that narrative verse tells a story.

Give each child **Copymaster 19 The Blind Men and the Elephant**. Read through the poem with the children and discuss what lesson it is teaching.

What did they think it was? 15-20min

Put the children into groups and give each group **Copymaster 20 What did they think it was?** One child should fill in the copymaster after the group have discussed what they should write beneath each heading.

Summary 

The children can compare their answers through class discussion.

Homework

Ask the children to think of an object or an animal which has many different parts. Make a list of the parts and write what someone might think the object/animal was if they had to close their eyes and could only touch one part at a time. You can read some of them out to the class without saying what the object/
animal is and see whether the children can guess it correctly.

18 Fables and parables

The Ant and the Beetle

An ant spent all summer running about in the fields and collecting grains of wheat and barley to store for the winter. A beetle watched the ant and was amazed that he worked so hard when the weather was good and many animals were having a rest.

Soon the winter came. The rain poured down and the beetle had no food. He was very hungry so he went to the ant to ask for something to eat.

"You should have gathered food in the summer. I worked hard because I knew there would be no food to get in the winter. You chose not to work so now you must go hungry."

The Good Samaritan

One day while Jesus was preaching he told the crowd that they should love their neighbours. One man asked Jesus who his neighbour was so Jesus told this parable.

"A man was travelling from the city of Jerusalem to Jericho. Some robbers attacked him and left him half-dead on the side of the road. Soon after, a priest came by. He saw the injured man but hurried by on the other side of the road. Not long after, another man came along the road. This man didn't want to get involved so he pretended that he had not seen the injured man.

The third man to pass by was a Samaritan. He saw that the man was hurt and needed help so the Samaritan took him to the nearest village and gave the innkeeper money to take care of him."

And Jesus asked, "Which of the three men was a good neighbour to the man who was attacked by the robbers?"

19 The Blind Men and the Elephant

It was six men of Hindostan,
To learning much inclined,
Who went to see an elephant,
(Though all of them were blind):
That each by observation
Might satisfy his mind.

The *first* approached the Elephant,
And happening to fall
Against his broad and sturdy side,
At once began to bawl;
"Bless me, it seems the Elephant,
Is very like a wall."

The *second*, feeling of his tusk,
Cried, "Ho! what have we here
So very round and smooth and sharp?
To me 'tis mighty clear
This wonder of an Elephant
Is very like a spear."

The *third* approached the animal
And happening to take
The squirming trunk within his hands,
Then boldly up and spake:
"I see," quoth he, "the Elephant
Is very like a snake."

The *fourth* stretched out his eager hand
And felt about the knee,
"What most this mighty beast is like
Is mighty plain," quoth he;
"'Tis clear enough the Elephant
Is very like a tree."

The *fifth* who chanced to touch the ear
Said, "Even the blindest man
Can tell what this resembles most;
Deny the fact who can,
This marvel of an Elephant
Is very like a fan."

The *sixth* no sooner had begun
About the beast to grope,
Than, seizing on the swinging tail
That fell within his scope,
"I see," cried he, "the Elephant
Is very like a rope."

And so these men of Hindostan
Disputed loud and long,
Each in his own opinion
Exceeding stiff and strong,
Though *each* was *partly* in the right
And all were in the wrong.

John Godfrey Saxe

What did they think it was?

The blind men	The part of the elephant they touched	What they thought it was
The first		
The second		
The third		
The fourth		
The fifth		
The sixth		

Which blind man was right?

What is the poem teaching us?

Sir Gawain and the Green Knight (1)

One Christmas, King Arthur held a feast at his court in Camelot. All his bravest knights were there and his beautiful Queen, Guinevere. Everyone was enjoying themselves when suddenly there was the sound of a horse's hooves outside. The great door flew open and into the hall rode a strange and frightening figure.

It was a man, so tall that everyone thought he was a giant. He wore green from head to foot, and the saddle and trappings of his horse were also green. His hair was bright green, his face was bright green, his hands were bright green! He carried with him a huge, sharp green axe.

The giant rode up to where Arthur was sitting and spoke in a loud, booming voice. "I have come here with a challenge. See this axe?" He held the huge axe up above his head. "Will any man here be brave enough to try to kill me with this axe? If he fails, then in one year's time he must come to find me and I will use this axe to kill him."

The knights and ladies of the court looked surprised and, for a while, no one stepped forward. Then a young knight named Sir Gawain said, "I will take your challenge."

"I am glad there is one brave knight amongst you," cried the giant. He leapt off his horse and handed the axe to Sir Gawain. He then knelt down and laid his neck bare so that Gawain could chop his head off. The great axe swung down and the giant's head came clean off his shoulders and bounced across the floor. For a second or two there was silence in the hall then the giant sprang up, picked up his head and got on his horse.

"Don't forget, Sir Gawain, you must come and find me in one year's time. Everyone in the north knows me. Just ask for the the Green Giant." And with that, he rode away.

Sir Gawain and the Green Knight (2)

1 What time of the year does the story take place?

____

2 Who comes to the court uninvited?

____

3 What is unusual about him?

____

4 What does the visitor challenge one of the knights to do?

____

5 Who accepts the challenge?

____

6 Write your own ending for the story.

____

____

____

____

____

____

____

____

____

Traditional tales

Choose one story opening, one character and one theme from below. Plan and write a traditional tale.

Story openings

Long, long ago …

In a far distant land …

Two mice lived at the edge of a cornfield …

There was once a boy called Jack …

Characters

Themes

- Your story can be about a long journey.
- In your story a poor man can get the better of a rich man.
- Your story can be a fable with animal characters.
- You can write a parable which teaches a lesson.

YEAR 3 TERM 3

Focus

In this section children will be given the opportunity to:

1 investigate/write story openings, characters and first person accounts within the context of adventure and mystery stories

2 investigate/write the differences between fact and fiction.

Content

Unit 1: Story openings
Unit 2: First person accounts
Unit 3: Fact and fiction
Unit 4: Playing with language

Reading List

'Betty Botter' from *Enjoying Poetry*, Macmillan Educational, 1981

Adams, Richard *Watership Down*, Penguin, 1973

Burgess, Melvin *The Earth Giant*, Puffin, 1997

Carroll, Lewis *Alice in Wonderland*

Coolidge, Susan *What Katy Did*

Davies, Jeffrey 'The Washing Machine' from *Enjoying Poetry*, Macmillan Educational, 1981

Kilworth, Garry *The Gargoyle*, Mammoth, 1997

Nichols, Judith 'Storytime' from *We Couldn't Provide Fish Thumbs*, Macmillan Children's Books, 1997

Scanell, Vernon 'Jason's Trial' from *We Couldn't Provide Fish Thumbs*, Macmillan Children's Books, 1997

Sewell, Anna *Black Beauty*

Assessment

Assessment Copymasters 34–5 are at the end of the section.

Copymaster 34 Adventure and mystery stories

Writing composition: the children are given the opportunity to continue a story.

Copymaster 35 Real life adventures

Writing composition: the children have the opportunity to base a story on factual information of the first manned moon landing.

National Literacy Strategy planner

This chart shows you how to find activities by unit to resource your term's requirements for text level work on fiction and poetry. The Learning Targets closely follow the structure of the fiction and poetry requirements for the term in the National Literacy Strategy document (pages 36–7). A few of the requirements are not covered. These are usually the ones that require extended reading or writing or comparison of several different texts.

YEAR 3 TERM 3

Range

Fiction and poetry:

- adventure and mystery stories
- stories by the same author
- humorous poetry
- poetry that plays with language, word puzzles, puns, riddles.

TEXT LEVEL WORK

COMPREHENSION AND COMPOSITION

Reading comprehension

Pupils should be taught:

1 to re-tell main points of story in sequence; to compare different stories; to evaluate stories and justify their preferences: Units 1–3;

2 to refer to significant aspects of the text, e.g. opening, build-up, atmosphere, and to know language is used to create these, e.g. use of adjectives for description: Units 1 and 2;

3 to distinguish between first and third person accounts: Unit 2;

4 to consider credibility of events, e.g. by selecting some real life adventures either written or retold as stories and comparing them with fiction: Unit 3;

5 to discuss (i) characters' feelings; (ii) behaviour, e.g. fair or unreasonable, brave or foolish; (iii) relationships, referring to the text and making judgements: Unit 1;

6 to compare forms or types of humour, e.g. by exploring, collecting and categorising form or type of humour, e.g. word play, joke poems, word games, absurdities, cautionary tales, nonsense verse, calligrams;

7 to select, prepare, read aloud and recite by heart poetry that plays with language or entertains; to recognise rhyme, alliteration and other patterns of sound that create effects: Unit 4;

8 to compare and contrast works by the same author, e.g. different stories, sequels using same characters in new settings, stories sharing similar themes;

9 to be aware of authors and to discuss preferences and reasons for these;

Writing composition

Pupils should be taught:

10 to plot a sequence of episodes modelled on a known story, as a plan for writing: Units 1 and 2;

11 to write openings to stories or chapters linked to or arising from reading; to focus on language to create effects, e.g. building tension, suspense, creating moods, setting scenes: Unit 1;

12 to write a first person account, e.g. write a character's own account of incident in story read: Unit 2;

13 to write more extended stories based on a plan of incidents and set out in simple chapters with titles and author details; to use paragraphs to organise the narrative: Unit 3;

14 to write book reviews for a specified audience, based on evaluations of plot, characters and language;

15 to write poetry that uses sound to create effects, e.g. onomatopoeia, alliteration, distinctive rhythms: Unit 4.

YEAR 3 TERM 3

UNIT 1

Story openings

Learning targets

On completion of this unit children should be able to:

1 ➾ refer to significant aspects of the text, e.g. opening, build up, atmosphere, and to know that language is used to create these, e.g. through use of adjectives

2 ➾ discuss (i) characters' feelings; (ii) behaviour, e.g. fair or unreasonable, brave or foolish; (iii) relationships, referring to the text and making judgements

3 ➾ write openings to stories or chapters linked to or arising from reading; to focus on language to create effects, e.g. building tension, suspense, creating moods and setting scenes.

Before you start

Background knowledge

This unit deals with plot and character in the context of mystery and adventure stories. Session 1 focuses on how a writer builds up suspense by 'stringing out' an event in a story so that the reader keeps reading to find out what is going to happen – the 'need to know' principle. Session 2 concentrates on character and how a reader can get to know characters in stories by how they act and react in a given situation.

Resources for Session 1

Copymasters 23a–b *The Earth Giant*, paper, pencils.

Resources for Session 2

Copymasters 24a–b *Watership Down*, Copymaster 25 If I were..., pencils, paper.

Links to other units

Learning Targets: Reading and Writing Key Stage 1 Section 2 Unit 1 on plot and Unit 2 on character and *Learning Targets: Grammar and Punctuation Key Stage 1* Section 4 on adjectives

Assessment indicators

- Can the children recognise how a writer builds up suspense?
- Can they discuss how characters act and react?

Teaching the sessions

Session 1 ① ③

Introduction 20-30min

Begin by discussing the adventure and mystery stories the children have read. What must a book have to be a 'mystery' or an 'adventure' story? It is not necessary to distinguish between the two at this stage as most children's adventure stories are woven around some sort of mystery, and most mystery stories have a strong element of adventure.

This is a good opportunity to bring in the 'need to know' principle, i.e. the reader just has to keep reading to find out what happens. Have the children experienced books that they 'could not put down'? What made them keep on reading?

Give each child **Copymasters 23a–b *The Earth Giant***, and read it through with them. In general terms, the extract centres on one event – Peter following his sister in the dead of night – where the details build up the mystery and suspense.

Base a whole class discussion on the following questions to bring out how the writer builds up the suspense.

- 'What word in the first sentence might make you want to read on?'
- 'Find two reasons why Peter is determined to follow his sister?'
- 'What is the first thing that Peter does?'
- 'Why do you think Amy casts "an anxious look back over her shoulder up at the house"?'
- 'As the reader, what questions are you asking at this point in the story?'
- 'How many times does Peter hide and what does he hide behind?'
- 'Why was the street "terrifying"?'
- 'When does Peter realise he has lost Amy?'
- 'As the reader, what questions are you asking at this point in the story?'

Explain to the children that the writer could simply have written: 'Peter got dressed and followed Amy into town. While he was hiding from a police car, he lost Amy.'

Which version is better? Why? Which version would make them want to go on reading? Why?

Brainstorming

20–30 min

Put the children into groups and give them one of the following scenarios to work on.

1. Two travellers have to make their way through a dark wood at night. They have a feeling they are not alone!
2. Two astronauts have landed on a strange planet and have travelled away from their spaceship in a small buggy to explore. The buggy breaks down. They have to get back to the spaceship on foot before their oxygen runs out.

The children have to explain what happens on the journey and list the words and phrases they would use to keep the reader in suspense. The reader must always be asking, 'What will happen next?'

Although they are working in groups, each child should make notes for their individual work later on.

Summary

10–15 min

The children can share their ideas through class discussion.

A dangerous journey

20 min

Based on their group work, each child can write the first draft of the journey. Emphasise that they are not writing the whole story, but an episode in a story which makes the reader want to go on reading.

Homework

The children can produce a final draft of their journey.

Session 2

2 3

Introduction

30 min

Give each child **Copymasters 24a–b *Watership Down***. Explain that the book is a whole series of adventures – some dangerous, some funny – which the rabbits experience in search of a new home. An important part of the story is the relationship between the rabbits who are very different characters. In this extract we see how Hazel and Bigwig, two of the rabbits, react when Fiver, another rabbit, is missing.

Read through the extract with the children and base a whole class discussion on the following questions to draw the children's attention to the characters.

- 'How does Hazel first realise Fiver has gone?'
- 'How do you know Hazel is worried?'
- 'How does Bigwig react when he realises Fiver is not in the burrow?'
- 'What is he going to do when he finds Fiver?'
- 'When Hazel says, "I'll hold him down while you kick him", do you think he really means it? What is he trying to get Bigwig to do?'
- 'How do you know that Bigwig is sensible and cautious?'
- 'How do you know Hazel is willing to risk danger to find Fiver?'
- 'When they find Fiver what surprising thing does he tell them?'
- 'What might make you want to go on reading?'

If I were...

20 min

Put the children into pairs and give each pair **Copymaster 25 If I were...** Explain to the children that they must imagine they were in both the situations on the copymaster and each of them must react in a different way: both responses can't be fearful/ brave/sensible, etc. They must make notes on:

- what they would do
- what they would say
- how they would feel.

Be on hand to discuss the 'work in progress'.

Summary

10 min

The children can share their work through class discussion. It will be interesting to find out whether the children wrote about how they would react or if they were able to imagine a different reaction.

Homework

Give each child Copymaster 24 *Watership Down* to take home. Ask them to write notes on what kind of characters they think Hazel, Bigwig and Fiver are.

The Earth Giant (1)

Peter and Amy are brother and sister. They usually get on very well but lately Amy has been acting very strangely. Peter knows she has a secret but she will not share it with him. He wakes up in the middle of the night and realises she is leaving the house.

He knew it was dangerous for his sister to go out alone … come to that it was dangerous for him at this time of night.

But this was an adventure.

Peter was sure of one thing. If she was brave enough to go out on her own, so was he. Besides … he wanted that secret.

He ran quietly to his window at the front just in time to see Amy walk round the side of the house. She was wrapped up with a coat and a woolly hat on as if it was the middle of winter, although it was July. She carried a bag in her hand. Just before she began up the drive she turned and cast an anxious look back over her shoulder up at the house. Peter darted back into the shadows … As fast as he could he pulled on his jeans and a thick sweater over his pyjamas, and ran downstairs.

On the road he hid behind the privet hedge and glanced up and down but he couldn't see her. Hurriedly he ran as quickly and as quietly as he could after her, pausing every now and then to peer ahead. At first he thought he'd missed her. But he saw a small figure up the road, crouching low by the side of a still car. She was peering behind her. Her face was white. Peter darted behind a car himself.

In a second Amy hurried on her way. Peter waited, and then followed on up the deserted street.

This was terrifying. The houses and trees, the familiar turns in the road all looked like ghosts, lifelessly waiting for something to happen. The

The Earth Giant (2)

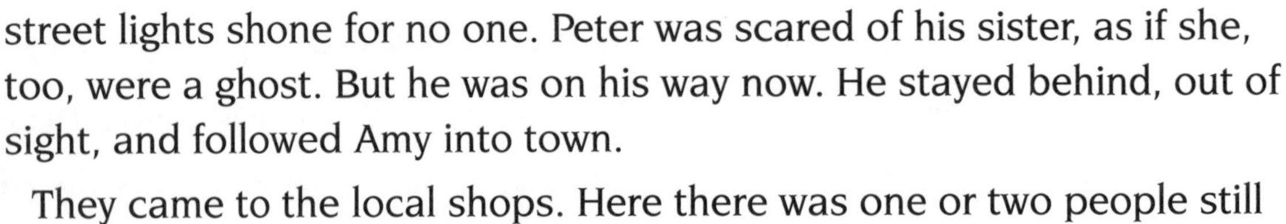

street lights shone for no one. Peter was scared of his sister, as if she, too, were a ghost. But he was on his way now. He stayed behind, out of sight, and followed Amy into town.

They came to the local shops. Here there was one or two people still about on the streets. A couple walked hurriedly past.

Amy saw them first, and dived behind a low wall. Peter got behind a hedge. Standing still, he shivered. He'd thought it would be warm, being summer, but at this hour of night it was cold. The couple walked past but before he could get out a man came up from behind and he had to wait in his hiding place while he passed. The man crossed the road and disappeared down a side alley. When Peter looked out again, Amy had disappeared.

He ran quietly forward. He had to hide again when a police car appeared, cruising slowly through the streets. When it went he ran on again, fearing to go too fast or make too much noise in case she was hiding nearby. But this time there was no little figure hurrying through the streets, no quick patter of footsteps on the pavement.

Amy had disappeared.

From *The Earth Giant* by Melvin Burgess

Watership Down (1)

A group of rabbits have had to leave their home and make a dangerous journey to find somewhere safe to live. They have found a warren and have been made welcome by the rabbits who live there but not everything is as it appears to be.

Hazel woke. He was in the burrow. He shivered. Why was there no warmth of rabbit bodies lying close together? Where was Fiver? He sat up. Near by, Bigwig was stirring and twitching in his sleep, searching for warmth, trying to press against another rabbit's body no longer there. The shallow hollow in the sandy floor where Fiver had lain was not quite cold: but Fiver was gone.

'Fiver!' said Hazel in the dark.

As soon as he had spoken he knew there would be no reply. He pushed Bigwig with his nose, butting urgently. 'Bigwig! Fiver's gone! Bigwig!'

Bigwig was wide awake on the instant and Hazel had never felt so glad of his sturdy readiness.

'What did you say?' What's wrong?'

'Fiver's gone.'

'Where's he gone?'

'... outside ... You know he wouldn't go wandering about in the warren. He hates it.'

'He's a nuisance, isn't he? He's left this burrow cold, too. You think he's in danger, don't you? You want to go and look for him?'

'Yes, I must. He's upset and over-wrought and it's not light yet. There may be enemies, whatever Strawberry says.'

Bigwig listened and sniffed for a few moments.

'It's very nearly light,' he said. 'There'll be light enough to find him by. Well, I'd better come with you, I suppose. Don't worry – he can't have gone far. But by the King's Lettuce! I won't half give him a piece of my mind when we catch him.'

'I'll hold him down while you kick him, if only we can find him. Come on!'

They went up the run to the mouth of the hole and paused together. 'Since our friends aren't here to push us,' said Bigwig, 'we may as well make sure the place isn't crawling with stoats and owls before we go out.'

Watership Down (2)

At that moment a brown owl's call sounded from the opposite wood. It was the first call, and by instinct they both crouched motionless, counting four heart-beats until the second followed.

'It's moving away,' said Hazel.

'How many field-mice say that every night, I wonder? You know the call's deceptive. It's meant to be.'

'Well, I can't help it,' said Hazel. 'Fiver's somewhere out there and I'm going after him. You were right, anyway. It *is* light – just.'

'Shall we look under the yew tree first?'

But Fiver was not under the yew tree. The light, as it grew, began to show the upper field, while the distant hedge and brook remained dark, linear shapes below. Bigwig jumped down from the bank into the field and ran in a long curve across the wet grass. He stopped almost opposite the hole by which they had come up, and Hazel joined him.

'Here's his line all right,' said Bigwig. 'Fresh, too. From the hole straight down towards the brook. He won't be far away.'

When raindrops are lying it is easy to see where grass has recently been crossed. They followed the line down the field and reached the hedge beside the carrot-ground and the source of the brook. Bigwig had been right when he said the line was fresh. As soon as they had come through the hedge they saw Fiver...

...Fiver sat up on his hind legs, cleaned his face with his paws and then, for the first time, looked directly at him.

'I'm going now,' he said. 'I feel very sad. I'd like to wish you well, Hazel, but there's no good to wish you well in this place. So just goodbye.'

'But where are you going, Fiver?'

'Away. To the hills, if I can get there.'

'By yourself, alone? You can't. You'd die.'

'You wouldn't have a hope, old chap,' said Bigwig. 'Something would get you before noon.'

'No', said Fiver very quietly. 'You are closer to death than I.'

From *Watership Down* by Richard Adams

25 If I were...

...trapped in a dark, cold dungeon

	Character 1	Character 2
What would I do?		
What would I say?		
How would I feel?		

...lost in the midde of a town at night

	Character 1	Character 2
What would I do?		
What would I say?		
How would I feel?		

YEAR 3 TERM 3

UNIT **2**

First person accounts

Learning targets

On completion of this unit children should be able to:

1 ➸ distinguish between first and third person accounts

2 ➸ write a first person account, e.g. write a character's account of an incident in a story.

Before you start

Background knowledge

This unit provides four story openings for the children to compare, two of these are written in the first person and two are in the third person. Suggestions are also given for using these extracts to revise the other aspects of story writing that the children have encountered.

The writing activities allow the children to turn a first person episode into the third person, and to write a character's own version of an incident in a story.

Resources for Session 1

Copymaster 26 First person stories, Copymaster 27 Third person stories, stories from the reading scheme, class library, etc.

Resources for Session 2

Copymasters 28a–b *The Gargoyle*.

Links to other units

Learning Targets: Reading and Writing Key Stage 1 Section 2, Unit 7 Session 3

Assessment indicators

- Can the children distinguish between first and third person stories?
- Can they rewrite stories from a different perspective, i.e. third person into first person; first person into third person?

Teaching the sessions

Session 1

Introduction

20–30min

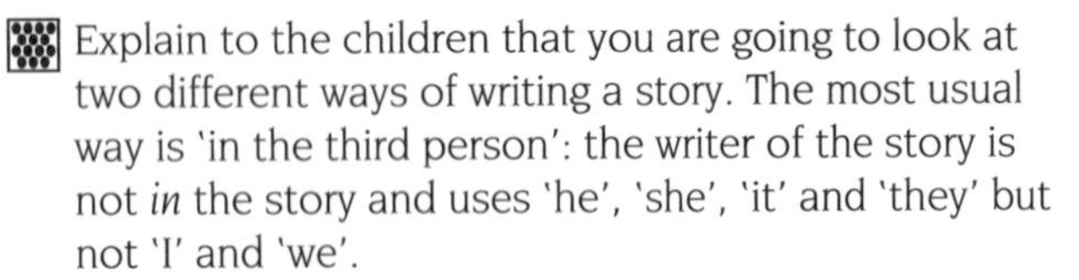

Explain to the children that you are going to look at two different ways of writing a story. The most usual way is 'in the third person': the writer of the story is not *in* the story and uses 'he', 'she', 'it' and 'they' but not 'I' and 'we'.

Another way to write a story is 'in the first person': the writer of the story is in the story and uses 'I' and 'we'. The writer may write 'he', 'she', 'it' or 'they' when writing about other characters but tells the story from their own point of view using 'I' or 'we'.

To ensure that the children are clear about the distinction, write some sentences on the board and ask them whether they would be found in a third or a first person story, e.g:

He waited until the house was quiet, then crept downstairs.

We were really looking forward to going on holiday.

She was very upset when she saw that her favourite toy was broken.

The dog limped over to the fire and lay down.

I wish I had never got a bicycle for my birthday.

Give each child **Copymaster 26 First person stories**. Explain to the children that these are the openings of two stories where the writer is in the story and is telling the story from his point of view.

Read the openings through with the children. They should have little difficulty in recognising that the writer of the stories is the 'I', and that the 'Davie' of the first extract is a boy/young man, but can they identify the 'I' of the second extract?

Give each child **Copymaster 27 Third person stories**. Again, read the extracts through and note the author's name. Ask the children if Susan Coolidge is *in* 'What Katy Did', and similarly, whether Lewis Carroll is *in* 'Alice in Wonderland'?

Use the four extracts to recap on what the children already know about narrative writing. You can discuss:

• story openings	What does each story opening do in terms of plot/character/setting/dialogue?
• plot	In terms of mystery/adventure stories, which of the openings leaves questions unanswered and would make the children want to read on?

• character	Which of the openings introduce a character or characters who the children think will figure largely in the story?
• setting	Which of the openings tells you about the setting of the story? How are the settings described, e.g. through the eyes of a character or by the writer?

Looking at stories

15-20min

Put the children into groups and give each group a selection of story books to look at. Ensure that there is a mix of first and third person accounts for each group.

Ask the children to look at their selection of books and list those which are third person stories and those which are first person stories. They should be able to tell by reading or skimming the first paragraph or two.

When they have done that, ask them to discuss which of the two types of stories they like best and why.

Summary

10-15 min

Discuss what the children found out about their books. Spend some time on exploring the reasons why they like first or third person stories best. This could lead on to a realisation that in a first person story, the reader usually only knows what the narrator of the story knows, whereas in a third person story, the author can let the reader know about things which the characters have not yet found out about. Some children find first person stories more exciting because the narrator can explain exactly what he/she is thinking/feeling/doing at the time.

Homework

Ask the children to turn the extract from 'Kidnapped!' into a third person story.

Session 2

Introduction

20min

Give each child **Copymasters 28a–b *The Gargoyle*** and read it through with the children. The children are going to use this third person account and write it as if they were Alex, i.e. as a first person account. To give the children the idea, you need to pick out various parts of the text and discuss them as a class.

'All seemed quiet in the room. Outside was pandemonium'. This is from the gargoyle's point of view. Alex has seen what he thinks is a large dog coming into his bedroom. How would he begin?

'The room remained still for some time, then the sound of sobbing came to the gargoyle and she could smell the musty odours of tears on human skin, of damp breath'. Again, this is what the gargoyle hears and smells. Might Alex say he kept very still, wondering what the dog was going to do? Would he admit he was crying? Would he mention the 'smell' of his tears.

Work through the extract in this way up to 'Boys my age don't cry.' To give them a start, write the first person account on the board as the children work through it.

Alex's story

Let the children continue the process of rewriting the extract as if Alex is telling the story. This is not an easy task and you should be on hand to help the children by asking them what they think Alex might say and pointing out any parts of the story that we know, as the reader, because we are seeing it from the point of view of the gargoyle.

Homework

The children can finish 'Alex's story' and illustrate it for homework.

First person stories

Kidnapped!

I will begin the story of my adventures with a certain morning, early in the month of June, the year of grace 1751, when I took the key for the last time out of the door of my father's house. The sun began to shine upon the summit of the hills as I went down the road; and by the time I had come as far as the manse, the blackbirds were whistling in the garden lilacs, and the mist that hung around the valley in the time of the dawn was beginning to arise and die away.

Mr Campbell, the minister of Essendean, was waiting for me by the garden gate, good man! He asked me if I had breakfasted; and hearing that I lacked for nothing, he took my hand in both of his and clapped it kindly under his arm.

"Well, Davie, lad," he said, "I will go with you as far as the ford, to set you on your way."

Robert Louis Stevenson

Black Beauty

The first place that I can well remember was a large pleasant meadow with a pond of clear water in it. Some shady trees leaned over it, and rushes and waterlilies grew at the deep end. Over the hedge on one side we looked into a ploughed field, and on the other we looked over a gate at our master's house, which stood by the roadside; at the top of the meadow was a plantation of fir trees, and at the bottom a running brook overhung by a steep bank.

Whilst I was young I lived upon my mother's milk, as I could not eat grass. In the daytime I ran by her side, and at night I lay down close by her. When it was hot, we used to stand by the pond in the shade of the trees, and when it was cold, we had a nice warm shed near the plantation.

Anna Sewell

Third person stories

What Katy Did

Katy's name was Katy Carr. She lived in the town of Burnet, which wasn't a very big town, but it was growing fast. The house she lived in stood on the edge of the town. It was a large square house, white, with green blinds, and had a porch in front, over which roses and clematis made a thick bower. Four tall locust-trees shaded the gravel path which led to the front gate. On one side of the house was an orchard; on the other side were wood piles and barns, and an ice-house. Behind was a kitchen garden sloping to the south; and behind that a pasture with a brook in it, and butternut-trees, and four cows, – two red ones, a yellow one with sharp tipped horns tipped with tin, and a dear little white one named Daisy.

Susan Coolidge

Alice in Wonderland

Alice was beginning to get very tired of sitting by her sister on the bank, and of having nothing to do: once or twice she had peeped into the book her sister was reading, but it had no pictures or conversations in it, "and what is the use of a book," thought Alice, "without pictures or conversation?"

So she was considering in her own mind (as well as she could, for the hot day made her feel very sleepy and stupid) whether the pleasure of making a daisy-chain would be worth the trouble of getting up and picking the daisies, when suddenly a White Rabbit with pink eyes ran close by her.

There was nothing so *very* remarkable in that; nor did Alice think it so *very* much out of the way to hear the Rabbit say to itself, "Oh dear! Oh dear! I shall be too late!"

Lewis Carroll

The Gargoyle (1)

At midnight, when there is a full moon, a stone gargoyle comes to life and wanders the streets of the town. On this occasion, it is spotted and chased. The gargoyle climbs in through an open window and meets a young boy named Alex.

All seemed quiet in the room. Outside was pandemonium.

The gargoyle could hear the police charging through the streets. There were distant shouts. Cars sped by, their lights clawing at the darkness in front of them. Gradually, all sounds faded away on the night.

The room remained still for some time, then the sound of sobbing came to the gargoyle and she could smell the musty odour of tears on human skin, of damp breath.

'Are you crying because of me?' asked the gargoyle, in her deep throaty tones. 'If you are, I shall leave.'

There was stillness for a moment, then a choked voice said, 'No – not because of you. I'm too upset to care about an old dog getting in my room. I wasn't crying though. You didn't hear me crying. I was just making a noise in my sleep. Boys my age don't cry.' There was another long silence then the words, 'How – how come you can talk?'

'How is it that *you* can talk?' countered the gargoyle.

'I learned when I was a baby,' said the voice in an aggrieved tone.

'Well, I learned from people,' said the gargoyle. 'People taught me to understand speech.' She paused before adding, 'I was never a baby. The mason carved me out of granite carried from a quarry far away. I think the block of stone must have been used for magic, because I come to life every full moon. Perhaps an ancient wizard used it as a table for his

28b The Gargoyle (2)

spells. Or spilled some enchanted potion on a rock. Who knows? Here I am and talking as well as any boy who learned as a baby.'

'I don't care about magic,' said the boy from the darkness of his bed. 'I just want my mum back home.'

'Good for you,' said the gargoyle. 'If I had a mother, I should want her back too.'

The boy sniffed then asked the gargoyle a question.

'If you're not a dog, what are you?'

'I'm a rather ugly gargoyle.'

The boy said, 'An ugly gargoyle? All gargoyles are ugly. I've seen them on churches. They're gross.'

'Is that short for grotesque? I believe I'm grotesque. I rather like being grotesque. It has dignity, that word. I could be absurd but I'm not. I'm grotesque. What are you?'

'I'm good-looking,' said the boy, emphatically. 'Nothing wrong with me.'

'There's nothing wrong with me, either,' said the gargoyle, huffily, 'apart from a little erosion.'

The boy seemed to hesitate before asking, 'What's erosion?'

From *The Gargoyle* by Garry Kilworth

YEAR 3 TERM 3

UNIT 3

Fact and fiction

Learning targets

On completion of this unit children should be able to:

1 ➸ consider the credibility of events, e.g. by selecting some real life adventures either written or retold as stories and comparing them with fiction

2 ➸ write more extended stories based on plan of incidents and set out in simple chapters with title and author; use paragraphs to organise the narrative.

Before you start

Background knowledge

To read an adventure story based on a real life experience and to consider the credibility of the events is something that would take children a considerable amount of time and rely heavily on their detailed knowledge of the events or on detailed research. As such, it is best tackled on an individual basis when a child has reached a competency in reading that will allow them to tackle such books, or as class topic based on an historic event or scientific discovery which forms part of another curricula area they are studying.

This unit concentrates on giving the basic facts of real life adventure for the children to use as the basis of a story which will allow them to draw on their knowledge of narrative style.

Resources for Session 1

Copymaster 29 The search for the city of Troy, Copymaster 30 Fact into fiction, pencils, paper.

Assessment indicators

- Can the children use a real life adventure as the basis for a story?

Teaching the sessions

Session 1 ❶ ❷

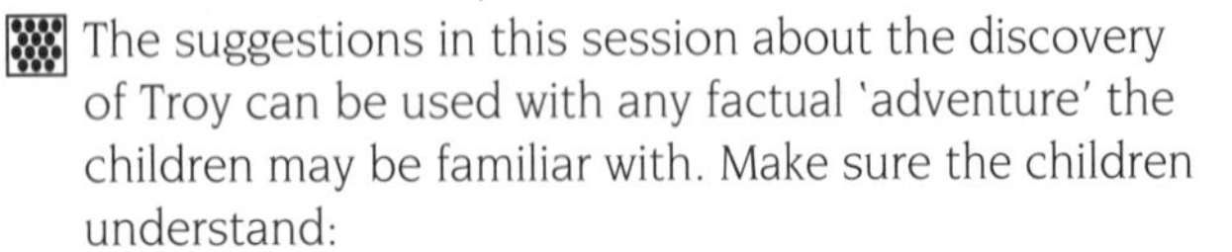

Introduction 20-30min

The suggestions in this session about the discovery of Troy can be used with any factual 'adventure' the children may be familiar with. Make sure the children understand:

- why the Greeks attacked Troy
- who Homer was
- that Homer wrote a long account of how Troy was destroyed in a book called *The Iliad*
- the fact that Troy was thought to be a legendary city before Heinrich Scheliemann discovered the ruins.

Give the children **Copymaster 29 The search for the city of Troy**, and read it through with the children. Discuss the following questions.

- 'What was Heinrich's Christmas present?'
- 'How did the present change his life?'
- 'Why did Heinrich learn Greek?'
- 'When did he set off to find Troy?'
- 'What is "archaeology"?'
- 'How many cities did he uncover?'
- 'What did he think belonged to Helen of Troy?'
- 'Which city did he think was Troy?'
- 'Was he right?'

Explain to the children that what they have just read is a factual account of what happened.

Fact into fiction 20-30min

Give each group **Copymaster 30 Fact into fiction**. They should discuss each point, with one child recording the group's decisions on the copymaster.

Check the children's work as they discuss the various elements of the story and show them how to use imaginary events within the framework of the facts, e.g. an accident could happen to one of the workman while digging, some of the 'treasures' could go missing.

If they have decided on a first person account, which character is telling the story?

Summary 10min

The groups can share their ideas by giving a potted version of their story's plot.

Writing the story 20-30min

See if the children can work together in groups to produce a story. A continuous prose account could be difficult but the children could produce a play script or captioned pictures.

The search for the city of Troy

Heinrich Scheliemann was only seven years old when his father gave him a Christmas present that would change his life. The present was a book about the ancient city of Troy and how it had been captured and burnt by the Greeks. Heinrich decided then and there that he would find this city and prove to the world that it was not just a legend.

Over the following years he taught himself Greek so he could read Homer's account, made a fortune as a merchant, and in 1871 set off with his Greek wife to find Troy. He employed 80 workmen and began to dig in the spot which fitted Homer's description of where the city was.

Heinrich did not know much about archaeology and very soon he was faced with masses of ruins which his workmen had uncovered. By the time they had finished, they had found nine cities built one on top of the other and Heinrich was convinced that the one at the bottom was Troy.

In 1873, after two years' work, they had uncovered 8700 golden objects – cups, vases, bracelets and a piece of magnificent jewellery that Heinrich was convinced had been worn by Helen of Troy.

Unfortunately, Heinrich was wrong! One of the cities that he had dug through was in fact Troy. The bottom city had been built much earlier and the piece of jewellery must have been worn by a princess or queen 1000 years before Helen of Troy was born. Nevertheless, Heinrich is known as the man who discovered the site of the ancient city of Troy as well as the older cities underneath.

Adapted from *The Reader's Digest Book of Strange Stories And Amazing Facts*

30 Fact into fiction

You are going to use the facts about the discovery of Troy as the basis of a story. You will need to think about and make notes on the things below.

Where will you start your story?

- When Heinrich is seven?
- When he arrives at Troy?
- When he discovers the cities?

List the characters in your story.

You might want to include one or more of the workmen so you will need to give them names.

Your reader will want to know what sort of people they are.

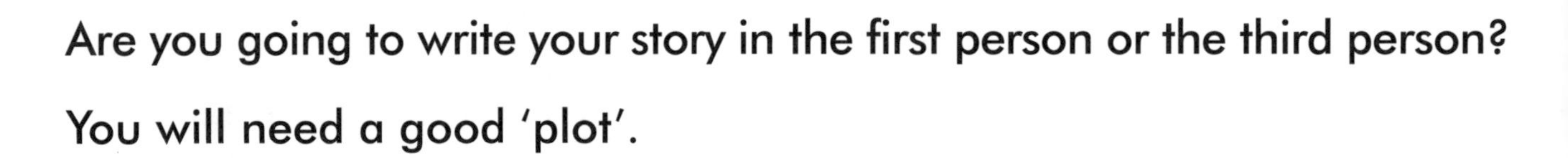

Are you going to write your story in the first person or the third person?

You will need a good 'plot'.

What happened:

- while they were digging
- when they found the last city
- when they found the jewellery
- when Heinrich realised he was wrong?

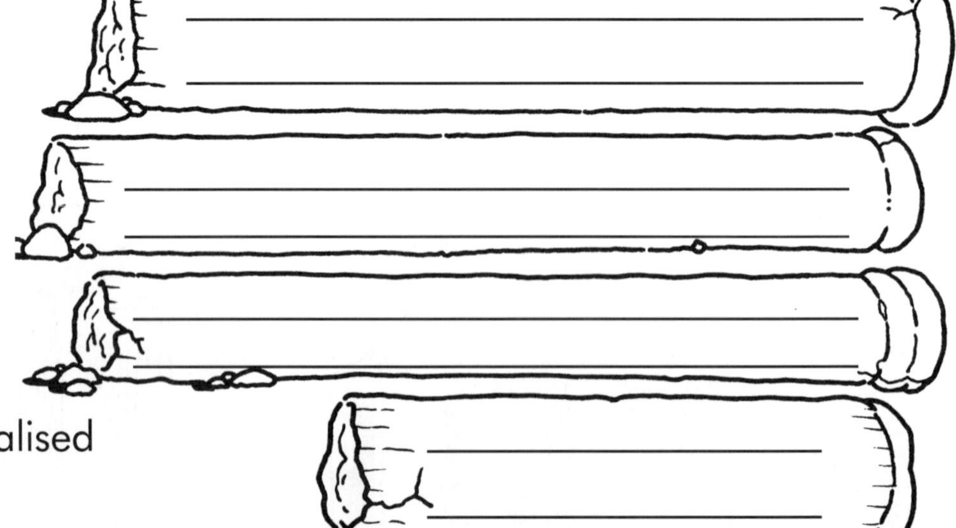

Remember! Your story needs to be exciting to keep the reader interested. You can imagine anything you like as long as you stick to the facts.

YEAR 3 TERM 3

UNIT 4

Playing with language

Learning targets

On completion of this unit children should be able to:

1 ➳ select, prepare, read aloud and recite by heart, poetry that plays with language or entertains

2 ➳ recognise rhythm, alliteration and other patterns of sound which create effects

3 ➳ write poetry that uses sound to create effects, e.g. onomatopoeia, alliteration and distinctive rhymes.

Before you start

Background knowledge

Children can have great fun with poems which play with language and as much time as possible ought to be given to letting them just read poems aloud and enjoy them. Most children actually like learning poetry and this should form an important part of the work from this unit.

Resources for Session 1

Copymaster 31 Jason's Trial, Copymaster 32 Storytime.

Resources for Session 2

Copymaster 33 Playing with words, pencils, felt-tip pens.

Links to other units

Learning Targets: Reading and Writing Key Stage 1 Section 1 Unit 6 on descriptive poetry

Assessment indicators

- Can the children prepare a poem to read aloud to the class?
- Can they recognise and use onomatopoeia and alliteration?

Teaching the sessions

Session 1 ①

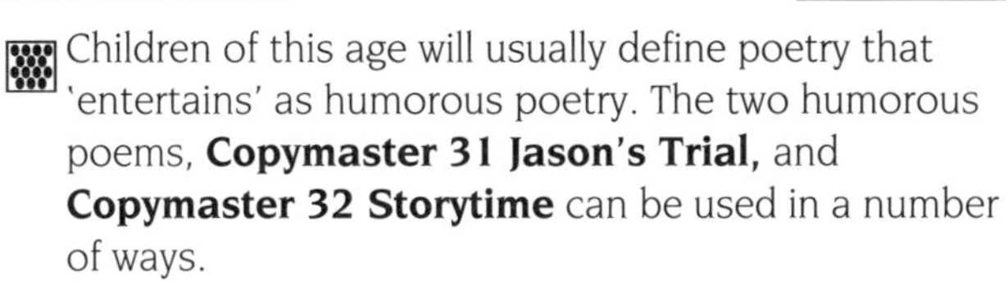

Introduction 20-25 min

Children of this age will usually define poetry that 'entertains' as humorous poetry. The two humorous poems, **Copymaster 31 Jason's Trial,** and **Copymaster 32 Storytime** can be used in a number of ways.

1 Use them in a whole class situation to be read and discussed. Ask the children:
   - 'Do you find the poems entertaining/funny?'
   - 'Can you say why?'
   - 'Which poem do you prefer?'
   - 'Why?'

2 Use one of the poems to show the children the various ways they can recite poetry. Different groups of children can read different verses or individual children can read the 'speaking part' within a poem.

It is, however, a good opportunity to see what the children can do on their own, and another option is to go straight into group work.

Performing poetry 20-30 min

Put the children into groups. Give some groups Copymaster 31 Jason's Trial and other groups Copymaster 32 Storytime.

Explain to the children that you want them to come up with a way of reading the whole of their poem to the rest of the class which involves each member of the group.

You will need to be on hand to help with organisation but, as far as possible, let the children see what they can do by themselves.

Summary 10-15 min

Each group can perform their poem for the class.

Homework

The children can learn their part of the poem by heart for a repeat performance without the aid of the copymasters.

Session 2 ② ③

Introduction 20-25 min

Another sort of poetry which children find entertaining is that which uses alliteration and/or onomatopoeia. Explain the following terms.

onomatopoeia	using words – often made up – which echo the sound being described
alliteration	using words which begin with the same sound or letter

Write the two words on the board and ask the children if they can think of any examples, e.g.

Onomatopoeia	Alliteration
buzz (bee)	Round the rugged rock
bang (drum)	The ragged rascal ran.
splash (something going into water)	
	She sells sea-shells
quack (a duck)	On the sea shore

Give the children **Copymaster 33 Playing with words** and read through the poems with the children:

The Washing Machine

Discuss the onomatopoeic words with the children. Can they pick them out? Do they think they are real words or made up? Do they look like other words that the children know?

Betty Botter

Which sound is repeated? Can the children pick out the words beginning with 'b'? This should help them to see that they do not need that many words to write an alliterative verse. A few can be repeated over and over again.

Writing poems

20-30min

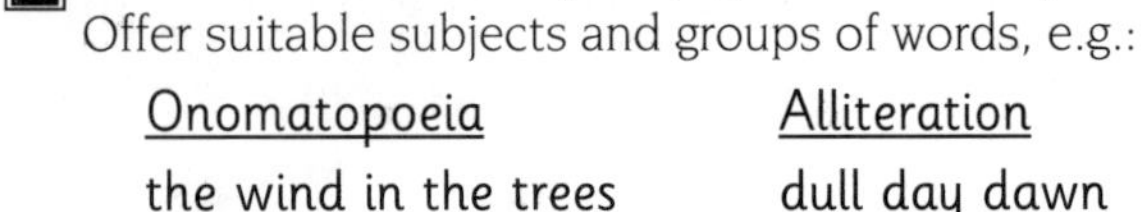

The children should try writing both sorts of poems. Offer suitable subjects and groups of words, e.g.:

Onomatopoeia	Alliteration
the wind in the trees	dull day dawn
traffic on a motorway	whistle whine
swimming	pen pat put

Homework

Poems can be written neatly and illustrated.

31 Jason's Trial

Jason was a football freak;
    He really loved the game:
To be a first-class footballer
    Was his one aim.

He practised every day and played
    Again each night in dream;
When he was twelve they chose him for
    The school's first team.

He was quite brilliant. Five years passed
    And – though rarely this occurs –
It seemed his dreams might all come true:
    He was given a trial by Spurs.

He played a blinder on that day;
    The spectators cheered and roared,
And after the match he was asked to appear
    Before the Selection Board.

The Chairman said, 'I've got the reports
    From our experts who watched you play:
Your speed and ball-control were fine;
    For tackling you get an A.

'And when our striker scored his goal
    You were the first to jump on his back,
And when *you* scored you punched the air
    Before you resumed the attack.

'So far, so good; but you were weak
    On the thing our lads do best;
It seems you hardly spat at all,
    So you failed the spitting-test.

'But don't despair. If you go home
    And practise every day
You still might learn to spit with style
    In the true professional way.'

Vernon Scannell

32 Storytime

Once upon a time, children,
there lived a fearsome dragon...

Please, miss
Jamie's made a dragon.
Out in the sandpit.

Lovely, Andrew.
Now this dragon
had enormous red eyes
and a swirling, whirling tale...

Jamie's dragon's got
yellow eyes, miss.

Lovely, Andrew.
Now this dragon was
as wide as a horse
as green as the grass
as tall as a house...

Jamie's would JUST *fit*
in our classroom, miss!

But he was a very friendly dragon...

Jamie's dragon ISN'T, *miss.*
He eats people, miss
Especially TEACHERS,
Jamie said.

Very nice, Andrew!
Now one day, children
this enormous dragon
rolled his red eye,
whirled his swirly green tail
and set off to find...

His dinner, miss!
Because he was hungry, miss!

Thank you, Andrew.

He rolled his red eye,
whirled his green tail,
and opened his wide, wide mouth
until

Please, miss
I did try to tell you, miss!

Judith Nichols

33 Playing with words

The Washing Machine

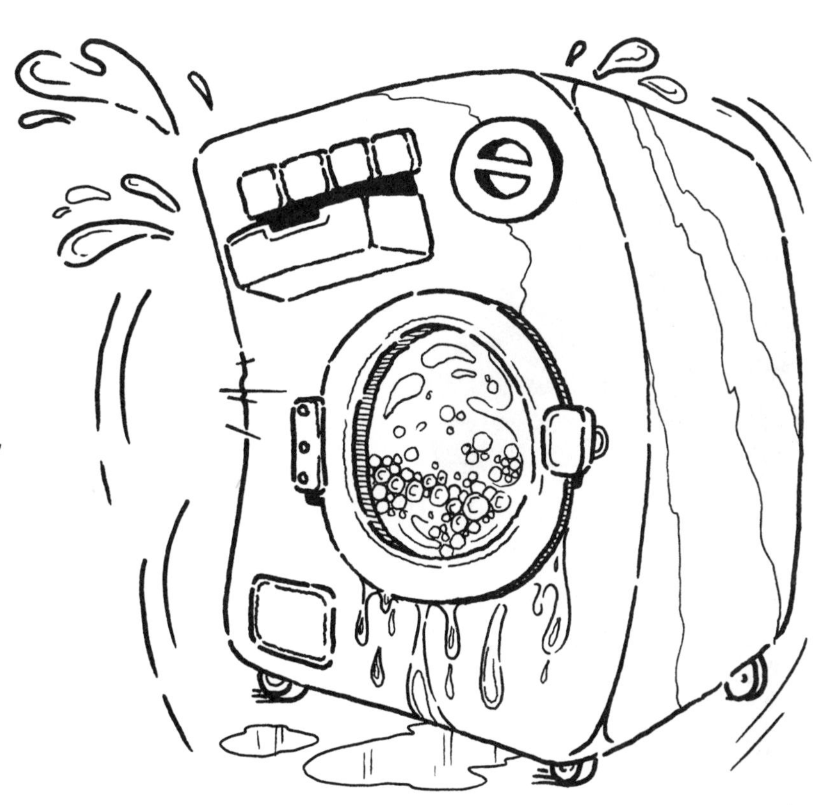

It goes fwunkety,
then slunkety,
as the washing goes around.

The water spluncheses,
and it sluncheses,
as the washing goes around.

As you pick it out it splocheses,
and it flocheses,
as the washing goes around.

By the end it schlopperies,
and then flopperies,
as the washing goes around.

Jeffery Davies

Betty Botter

Betty Botter bought some butter,
But, she said, the butter's bitter;
If I put it in my batter
It will make my batter bitter,
But a bit of better butter's
Bound to make my batter better.
So she bought a bit of butter
Better than her bitter butter,
And she put it in her batter
And the batter wasn't bitter.
So 'twas better Betty Botter
Bought a bit of better butter.

Anon

Adventure and mystery stories

This is the beginning of a story called *The King in the Forest* by Michael Morpurgo.

Deep in the forest there lived a charcoal-burner and his son Tod. They were poor people but if they worked hard there was just enough food to feed themselves, their cow and their donkey.

Once a month Tod's father would load up the donkey with charcoal and take it into town to sell in the market, and so Tod would be left on his own to milk the cow, chop the wood and keep the charcoal ovens burning.

One fine morning with his father gone into town, Tod was out chopping wood when he heard the sound of hunting horns echoing through the forest. The King would be out hunting again as he often was.

As the baying of the hounds came ever closer Tod looked up from his chopping. Something was moving at the edge of the forest, something white and small...

What do you think happened next?

Continue the story and make it as exciting as you can.

Real life adventures

One of the most exciting real life adventures ever took place on 21 July 1969 when men landed on the moon.

Here are some of the facts you need to know.

- The spacecraft was called Apollo 11.
- Apollo 11 had two parts. One was called Columbia and the other was called Eagle.
- The three men on the spacecraft were Neil Armstrong, Buzz Aldrin and Michael Collins.
- Michael Collins stayed in one part of the spaceship called Columbia and went around the moon while Armstrong and Aldrin went down onto the moon in Eagle.
- The Eagle almost landed in a large crater but Armstrong managed to get it down safely.
- They landed at a place called the Sea of Tranquillity.
- Neil Armstrong was the first man to set foot on the moon.

Imagine you were one of the three astronauts. Write a story about your trip to the moon. Use as many of the facts above as you can.

Remember to write about what happened and how you felt. Make it as exciting as you can.

YEAR 4 TERM 1

Focus

In this section children will be given the opportunity to:

1 investigate/write settings and characters in historical stories
2 investigate/write play scripts within an historical context
3 investigate/write poems on similar themes.

Content

Unit 1: Characters
Unit 2: Play scripts
Unit 3: Poetry writing

Reading List

Carroll, Lewis *Alice in Wonderland*

Causley, Charles 'I saw a Jolly Hunter' from *Figgie Hobbin*, Macmillan

Dane, Clemence A *Dramatisation of Alice's Adventures in Wonderland and Through the Looking Glass*, French, 1948

Masefield, John 'Reynard the Fox'

Mooney, Bel *The Stove Haunting*, Mammoth, 1998

Stevens, James 'The Snare'

Assessment

Assessment Copymasters 46–7 are at the end of the section.

Copymaster 46 Historical stories

Writing composition: gives the children the opportunity to write character sketches based on physical description and personality to evoke a required response in the reader.

Copymaster 47 Play scripts

Writing composition: this gives the children the opportunity to convert a prose passage into a play script with scene, characters, stage directions and dialogue.

National Literacy Strategy planner

This chart shows you how to find activities by unit to resource your term's requirements for text level work on fiction and poetry. The Learning Targets closely follow the structure of the fiction and poetry requirements for the term in the National Literacy Strategy document (pages 38–9). A few of the requirements are not covered. These are usually the ones that require extended reading or writing or comparison of several different texts.

YEAR 4 TERM 1

Range

Fiction and poetry:

- historical stories and short novels
- play scripts
- poems based on common themes, e.g. space, school, animals, families, feelings, viewpoints.

TEXT LEVEL WORK

COMPREHENSION AND COMPOSITION

Reading comprehension

Pupils should be taught:

1 to investigate how settings and characters are built up from small details and how the reader responds to them: Unit 1;

2 to identify the main characteristics of the key characters, drawing on the text to justify views, and using the information to predict actions: Unit 2;

3 to explore chronology in narrative using written or other media texts, by mapping how much time passes in the course of the story, e.g. noticing where there are jumps in time, or where some events are skimmed over quickly, and others told in detail;

4 to explore narrative order: identify and map out the main stages of the story: introductions → build ups → climaxes or conflicts → resolutions;

5 to prepare, read and perform play scripts; compare organisation of scripts with stories – how are settings indicated, story lines made clear? Unit 2;

6 to chart the build-up of a play scene, e.g. how scenes start, how dialogue is expressed, and how scenes are concluded: Unit 2;

7 compare and contrast poems on similar themes, particularly their form and language, discussing personal responses and preferences: Unit 3;

8 to find out more about popular authors, poets, etc. and use this information to move onto more books by favourite writers;

Writing composition

Pupils should be taught:

9 to use different ways of planning stories, e.g. using brainstorming, notes, diagrams;

10 to plan a story identifying the stages of its telling;

11 to write character sketches, focusing on small details to evoke sympathy or dislike: Unit 1;

12 to write independently, linking own experience to situations in historical stories, e.g. *How would I have responded? What would I do next?* Unit 1;

13 to write play scripts, e.g. using known stories as a basis: Unit 2;

14 to write poems based on personal or imagined experience, linked to poems read. List brief phrases and words, experiment by trimming or extending sentences; experiment with powerful and expressive verbs: Unit 3;

15 to use paragraphs in story writing to organise and sequence the narrative.

YEAR 4 TERM 1

UNIT 1

Characters

Learning targets

On completion of this unit children should be able to:

1 ➤➤ investigate how settings and characters are built up from small details

2 ➤➤ identify the key characteristics of the key characters, drawing on the text to justify views, and using the information to predict actions

3 ➤➤ write character sketches focusing on small details to evoke sympathy or dislike

4 ➤➤ write independently, linking own experience to situations in historical stories, e.g. How would I have responded? What would I do next?

Before you start

Background knowledge

This unit deals with character and setting within the context of historical novels and stories. Session 1 focuses on the detail the writer includes to bring the past alive for the reader, particularly the minute description of setting, and asks the children to make judgements about the characters within that setting. Session 2 looks at the characters' actions and asks the children to put themselves into the given situation and imagine how they would respond.

Resources for Session 1

Copymasters 36a–b *The Stove Haunting*, Copymaster 37 Descriptive detail, illustrated factual historical books, pencils, paper.

Resources for Session 2

Copymasters 36a–b *The Stove Haunting*, factual history books, pencils, paper.

Links to other units

Learning Targets: Reading and Writing Key Stage 1 Section 2 Unit 2 on character and Unit 3 on setting

Assessment indicators

- Can the children assess the characters' appearance and personality from reading?
- Can they put themselves into a character's situation and judge how they might behave/feel?

Teaching the sessions

Session 1

Introduction — 20-30 min

Begin by discussing any historical stories the children may have read. This is perhaps not the usual reading diet of children this age but they may appreciate the concept because of historical adventures on television.

Discuss what elements they think are necessary in a historical story.

- 'Is it set in the past, present or future?'
- 'Do all, some or none of the characters need to have been 'real' people?
- 'Has everything in the story really happened?'

This is a good opportunity to point out the difference between historical 'fact' and historical 'fiction'. Historical fiction draws on factual knowledge of a particular time and place, but imaginary characters and events can be incorporated.

Give each child **Copymasters 36a–b *The Stove Haunting*** and read it through with them. At this stage, focus the children's attention on the type of place the cottage is. Would they like to live there? Why not? Ask them to pick out words and phrases which the writer has used to describe the cottage in detail and to give the reader a realistic impression of the poverty in which some people lived in the early nineteenth century.

Descriptive detail — 20-30 min

Give each group a photocopy of **Copymaster 37 Descriptive detail**. One child from each group can complete the copymaster based on group discussion.

Summary — 10-15 min

Compare the descriptive detail each group noted through class discussion. Write a list on the board of the words and phrases they added to the description, discussing any which seem inappropriate.

An historical setting — 20-30 min

Choose a place, such as a building/location from the historical period the children are studying and ask them to write a detailed description. They must imagine that they have travelled back in time to that place (be it a mediaeval castle, a Tudor battlefield, or an Elizabethan ship) and describe it through their 'modern' eyes. Let the children look at factual historical books to stimulate their writing. Remind them that this is to be written as a setting for a story.

Homework

The children can complete their descriptive work and illustrate it.

Session 2

Introduction

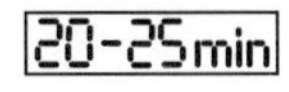

Using **Copymasters 36a–b *The Stove Haunting*** as a stimulus, focus the children's attention on the characters.

Begin by asking who the characters are in the extract and what the children know about them. Can they distinguish between characters who actually 'appear' and those who are simply referred to?

Daniel	a twentieth-century boy who has been transported back into the nineteenth century as a kitchen boy
George	Daniel's friend
Samuel Smith	lives in the house which George and Daniel are visiting; obviously George's friend
'a woman'	Samuel Smith's wife
'a child of about eighteen months'	Samuel's youngest child
'Young William'	Samuel's son
Rose	Samuel's daughter
'the twins'	the Smith's other children

Take each character in turn and ask the children to look for any clues in the extract as to what sort of people they are.

Daniel	compassionate – the crying baby 'pierced Daniel to the heart'
George	caring/considerate – when Daniel stumbled he was 'quickly steadied by George's brotherly arm'; he refuses Samuel's beer and bread because they have so little
Samuel Smith	friendly – when George goes into the house 'a man clasped him warmly by the hand'; generous – he offers George beer and food although he cannot afford to do so
Mrs Smith	exhausted and defeated by her circumstances – 'The mother raised exhausted eyes to the visitors, tried to smile but failed.'

Discuss how the children react to:

- the fact that the parents seem not to notice the baby crying
- Mrs Smith's obvious pride in William and Rose.

How do the children react to the characters in general? Has the author managed to evoke their pity and sympathy, perhaps even horror at the way they are forced to live?

How would I feel?

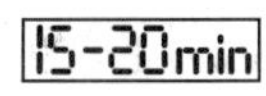

The characters in the extract seem to be bearing up under very difficult circumstances. Explain that these characters are very poor because they are paid an incredibly low wage for long hours of work on rich farmers' lands.

Put the children into groups and ask them to discuss how they might behave if they were very poor farm workers, living in the conditions detailed in the passage, in the early nineteenth century.

Be on hand to 'guide' the discussion so the children do not think their problems would be solved by 'shooting the farmer'! How would they realistically feel? What could they realistically do?

Summary

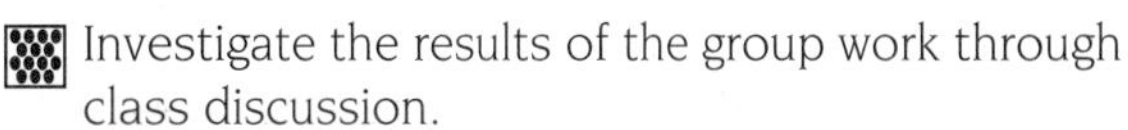

Investigate the results of the group work through class discussion.

Character sketches

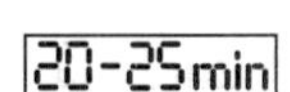

Ask the children to choose a location from an historical period to write a detailed 'setting'. They should write a detailed description of a character in a similar context.

Alternatively, they can choose either Rose or William from *The Stove Haunting* and, using what they know of their family and circumstances, write a detailed character sketch.

Homework

Character sketches can be finished for homework.

The Stove Haunting (1)

Daniel has mysteriously been taken back in time and finds himself as a kitchen boy in the year 1835. One evening he is taken by his friend George to visit Samuel Smith who lives in the nearby village of Winterstoke.

They must have walked for about a mile and a half, and it had grown quite dark when George suddenly turned off the main track. The narrower path they were now on was very stony, and once or twice Daniel stumbled, but he was quickly steadied by George's brotherly arm. There was a smell of dung, smoke and rotting vegetation in the air. George stopped and held Daniel's arm with fingers that dug into his flesh.

'Listen!' he cried hoarsely.

A child was crying. The little voice rose and fell in the darkness, dying away on the light, cold wind. Then it rose again, and something about the tone pierced Daniel to his heart. He had heard babies cry before – outside supermarkets, or in shops when their parents refused them a toy or sweets – but this sound was different. There was such a note of pain, of terrible hopelessness in this child's cry, that it made Daniel shudder and feel, for some inexplicable reason, as if it were his fault.

At the end of the path was a tiny house, this one truly like a hut. The walls seemed to be made of dirt or clay, and they gaped with holes. The thatched roof dropped down to the ground on each side like dirty hair round a poor and grubby face. There were holes in the thatch too, and the two small windows on each side of the door were stuffed with sacking. In the pale light of the moon the little building looked bleak and cold. And all the time, the desperate crying went on, coming from within.

The door opened as soon as George knocked, and a man clasped him warmly by the hand. He nodded down at Daniel and drew them both inside, leading them across to two rough wooden boxes that served for chairs on each side of the fire.

The Stove Haunting (2)

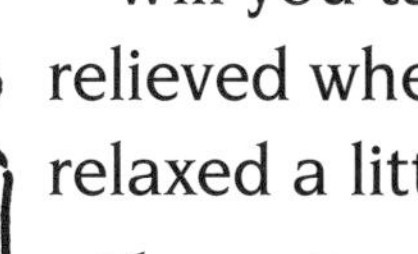

'Will you take a drop of beer, George?' the man asked. He looked relieved when George shook his head and his hunched shoulders relaxed a little.

The cottage consisted of one small room, lit by two candles. An iron pot was hanging by a black chain over the open fire. The floor was trodden earth but two dirty sacks had been laid in front of the fire as a makeshift carpet. On a shelf in the wall by the fire stood two onions, placed as if they were precious objects. On the rough wooden table, which was the only proper furniture in the room, together with the bench which stood by it, was half a loaf of dark grainy bread and an earthenware pot with a knife stuck in it. The man pointed to these. 'So, will you take a bit o' bread and lard?' he asked. George shook his head again.

In one corner of the room, just where the tiny staircase curled up behind the fire, a woman sat on a pile of sacks on the floor. In her arms was a child of about eighteen months, and it was still crying. Neither parent seemed to notice the sound. It was as if they had grown so used to it that they did not bother to make hushing sounds, or even rock the baby any more. The mother raised exhausted eyes to the visitors, tried to smile, but failed.

'I hope you're well, George?' she managed to whisper at last, as if it were almost too much of an effort to speak.

'How's the little un?' he asked instead of replying.

The mother seemed to shrink back on the sacks, and now made pathetic rocking movements with her bony arms.

'Bad, George, there's a fever now and he's been coughing as if his little chest would break in two.'

'And the others?' asked George.

'Not so bad, thanks be. Young William's started work now, and Rose went out stone-picking with the gang; and the twins done well with the lazin'.' She pointed proudly to the small sack of flour, made from the grains of wheat that family had managed to pick up after harvest, to make their bread with during the long winter.

From *The Stove Hunting* by Bel Mooney

37 Descriptive detail

Read through the extract from *The Stove Haunting* and complete this copymaster.

Outside

Write the words and phrases the writer uses to describe the outside of the house.

Write some words and phrases of your own to add to this description.

Inside

Write the words and phrases the writer uses to describe the inside of the house.

Write some words and phrases of your own to add to this description.

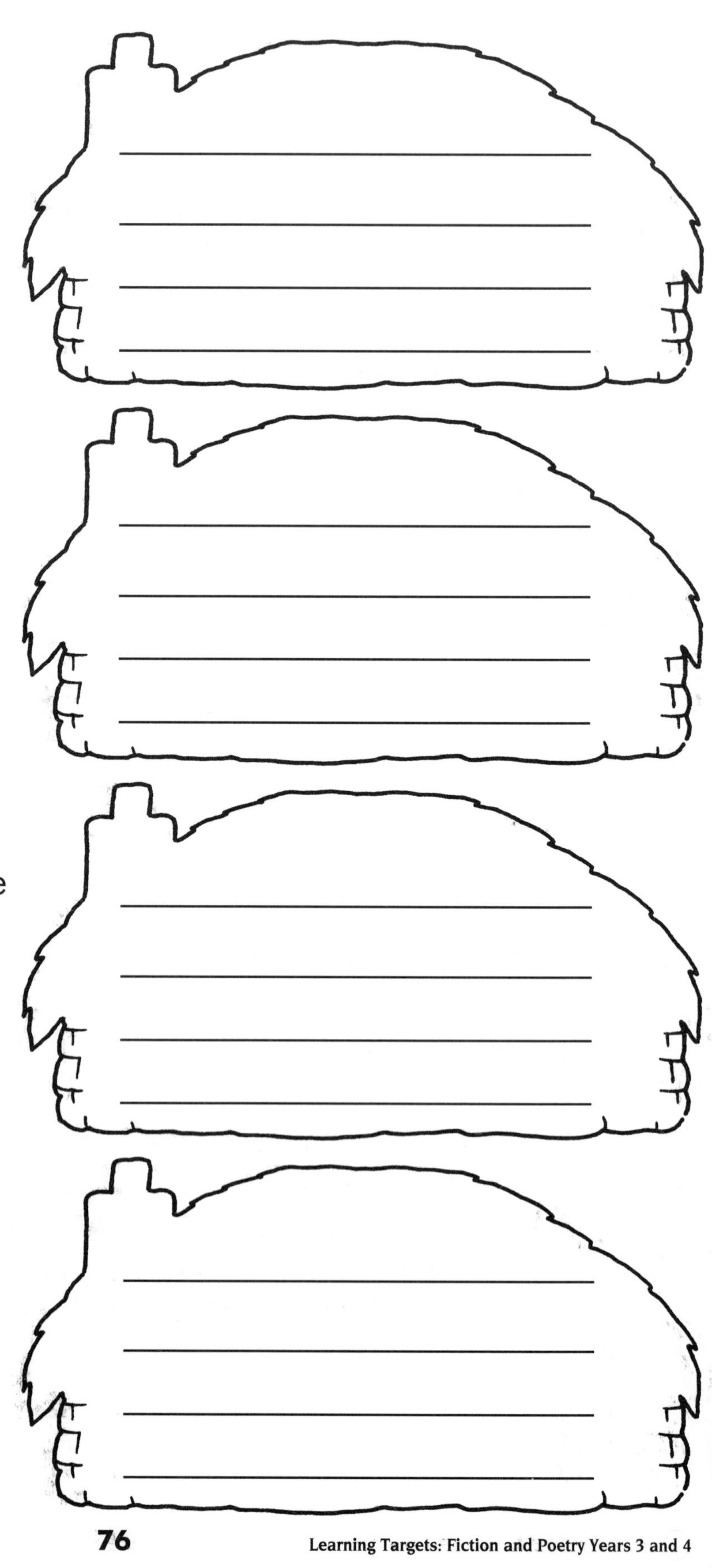

YEAR 4 TERM 1
UNIT 2

Play scripts

Learning targets

On completion of this unit children should be able to:

1 ➤➤ prepare, read and perform play scripts; compare organisation of scripts with stories – how settings are indicated, story lines made clear

2 ➤➤ write play scripts, using known stories as a basis.

Before you start

Background knowledge

This unit is a continuation of the work on plays at Key Stage 1. Session 1 gives the children the opportunity to look at an extract from a well-known story and the corresponding play script on which they can model their own work. Session 2 provides the children with another extract from the same source to rewrite as a play script, focusing on setting, characters, props and dialogue.

Resources for Session 1

Copymasters 38a–b *Alice in Wonderland*, Copymaster 39 *Alice in Wonderland* – a play, Copymaster 40 Notes for a play, pencils.

Resources for Session 2

Copymaster 40 Notes for a play, Copymasters 41a–b Who stole the tarts?

Links to other units

Learning Targets: Reading and Writing Key Stage 1 Section 3 Unit 1 on plot, Unit 2 on setting and Unit 3 on characters

Assessment indicators

- Can the children identify various parts of a continuous prose extract that they would use for scenes/props, stage directions and dialogue in a play script?
- Can they prepare and read/act a play script?

Teaching the sessions

Session 1

Introduction (20–30 min)

Begin by discussing the idea of a 'play' with the children. Can they remember the work they did on plays at Key Stage 1? How does a play script look different 'on the page' to a story? What is the difference between reading a story and seeing that story acted on the stage or television?

Explain to the children that you are going to read an extract from a story and then look at the same extract written as a play script.

Give each child **Copymasters 38a–b *Alice in Wonderland*** and read it through with the children. Some of them may know the story very well but you may have to explain the background for others. Ensure that the children know:

- that the Cheshire cat appears and disappears at will and sometimes only part of him appears
- what is entailed in playing croquet.

When you have discussed the extract and the children are clear as to what is going on, give each child **Copymaster 29 Alice in Wonderland – a play**. Explain that this is exactly the same part of the story but you would watch it on stage or television, rather than read it in a book. Ask the following sorts of questions.

- 'What differences can you find?'
- 'Why do you think the play script is shorter?'
- 'Why does Alice say less in the script than in the story?'

The result of the discussion should be that the children realise that because we can 'see' the actions of the characters and 'hear' how they say their words we do not need so much detail on the page. It should also reinforce that the narrative part of the story can be used for stage directions and instructions about how characters move and speak.

What do we need? (20 min)

Working in groups of four, give each group **Copymaster 40 Notes for a play**. One child can fill in the copymaster based on group discussion.

Explain that they must look carefully at the play script and write: a description of the scene (set) they would need for this part of the play, a list of characters, and a list of props.

Summary (10–15 min)

The children can compare their work through class discussion. The 'set' might well be the most problematic but this has been deliberately left vague so the children come to realise that not every detail they need will necessarily be in the story. They are allowed to use their imagination within the given context.

How would I play... ? 20-25 min

Ask the children to prepare the script to act for the rest of the class. At this stage they should concentrate on allotting parts and working out movements.

Homework

The children should learn their lines for homework.

Session 2

Introduction 25 min

Give some time at the beginning of the session for each group to act their 'play'.

Recap on what a play script needs, i.e.:

- scene (set)
- stage directions – for actions/to indicate props/ to indicate how words are spoken
- dialogue.

Give each child **Copymasters 41a–b Who stole the tarts?** and read through it with the children. Explain that they are going to work in groups and turn this extract into a play script.

What do we need? 30 min

After reading through the copymaster with the children, you could go on to discuss this activity with the whole class, but it may be more profitable to put them into groups immediately and be on hand to discuss individual problems. Copymaster 40 Notes for a play, will help each group to focus on how the set would look, the characters needed (speaking and non-speaking) and the props those characters will need.

When the children have resolved these issues, they can move on to consider the dialogue. The most problematic area will be when Alice is 'thinking' or 'talking to herself'. How will this be conveyed to an audience? Alice could:

- speak directly to the audience (an aside)
- say these things to another character.

If children prefer the second option, they will need to decide which character she is talking to and possibly invent some dialogue for that character to speak in reply.

While the children are sorting out and writing the dialogue, prompt them to include stage directions by referring them back to the text. Ask questions such as:

- 'How does Alice say, "What are they all doing?"'
- 'Where is Alice when she takes the squeaking pencil away?'
- 'Who is not on the set at the beginning but comes in towards the end?'

You will probably need more than this session for the children to complete the work. They should be given the opportunity to act it out for the rest of the class, and possibly to word process their script, listing the characters and who is playing them.

Homework

At the appropriate stage, homework can be:

- drawing and annotating the set
- drawing and annotating the character the child is playing including details of costume and props
- learning their lines.

Alice in Wonderland (1)

Alice had followed a white rabbit and found herself in Wonderland where she has many strange adventures. Here she is playing croquet with the Queen of Hearts using a flamingo as a mallet and rolled up hedgehogs for croquet balls! The Queen's soldiers have to bend over to make the hoops to hit the balls through.

She was looking about for some way of escape, and wondering whether she could get away without being seen, when she noticed a curious appearance in the air: it puzzled her very much at first, but after watching it a minute or two, she made it out to be a grin, and she said to herself, "It's the Cheshire Cat: now I shall have somebody to talk to."

"How are you getting on?" said the Cat, as soon as there was mouth enough for it to speak with.

Alice waited till the eyes appeared, and then nodded. "It's no use speaking to it," she thought, "till its ears have come, or at least one of them." In another minute the whole head appeared, and then Alice put down her flamingo, and began an account of the game, feeling very glad she had some one to listen to her. The Cat seemed to think that there was enough of it now in sight, and no more of it appeared.

"I don't think they play at all fairly," Alice began, in a rather complaining tone, "and they all quarrel so dreadfully one can't hear oneself speak – and they don't seem to have any rules in particular; at least, if there are, nobody attends to them – and you've no idea how confusing it is all the things being alive; for instance, there's the arch I've got to go through next walking about at the other end of the ground – and I should have croqueted the Queen's hedgehog just now, only it ran away when it saw mine coming."

Alice in Wonderland (2)

"How do you like the Queen?" said the Cat in a low voice.

"Not at all," said Alice: "she's so extremely—" Just then she noticed that the Queen was close behind her listening: so she went on, "—likely to win, that it's hardly worth finishing the game."

The Queen smiled and passed on.

"Who *are* you talking to?" said the King, coming up to Alice, and looking at the Cat's head with great curiosity.

"It's a friend of mine – a Cheshire Cat," said Alice: "allow me to introduce it."

"I don't like the look of it at all," said the King: "however, it may kiss my hand if it likes."

"I'd rather not," the Cat remarked.

"Don't be impertinent," said the King, "and don't look at me like that!" He got behind Alice as he spoke.

"A cat may look at a king," said Alice. "I've read that in some book, but I don't remember where."

"Well, it must be removed," said the King very decidedly, and he called to the Queen, who was passing at that moment. "My dear! I wish you would have this cat removed!"

The Queen had only one way of settling all difficulties, great or small. "Off with his head!" she said, without even looking round.

"I'll fetch the executioner myself," said the King eagerly, and he hurried off.

From *Alice in Wonderland* by Lewis Carrol

Alice in Wonderland – a play

SCENE: ALICE IS PLAYING CROQUET WITH THE QUEEN.

[*the Cheshire Cat appears*]

Cheshire Cat: How are you getting on?

Alice: I don't think they play at all fairly, and they all quarrel so dreadfully one can't hear oneself speak.

Cheshire Cat: [*in a low voice*] How do you like the Queen?

Alice: Not at all. She's so extremely...

[*The Queen suddenly enters. Alice, noticing her, concludes her sentence*].

...likely to win that it's hardly worth finishing the game.

[*The Queen smiles and exits. The King enters between Alice and the Cheshire Cat.*]

King: Who are you talking to?

Alice: It's the Cheshire cat – a friend of mine.

King: I don't like the look of it at all. However, it may kiss my hand if it likes.

Cheshire Cat: I'd rather not.

King: Don't be impertinent! And don't look at me like that!

[*frightened, he crosses to the left of Alice*]

Alice: A cat may look at a king.

King: It must be removed.

[*the Queen enters*]

Queen: Off with its head! Executioner!

Clemence Dane

40 Notes for a play

The set

What will the stage look like?

Draw and write about it here.

The characters

Make a list of the characters you will need.

Props

What will your characters need while they are on stage?

Who stole the tarts? (1)

In Wonderland, the Knave of Hearts has been accused of stealing some tarts. Alice finds herself at the trial where the Knave has to answer the charges.

The King and Queen were seated on their throne when they arrived, with a great crowd assembled about them – all sorts of little birds and beasts, as well as the whole pack of cards: the Knave was standing before them, in chains, with a soldier on each side to guard him: and near the King was the White Rabbit, with a trumpet in one hand, and a scroll of parchment in the other. In the very middle of the court was a table, with a large dish of tarts upon it: they looked so good, that it made Alice quite hungry to look at them – "I wish they'd get the trial done," she thought, "and hand round the refreshments!" But there seemed to be no chance of this, so she began looking about her, to pass away the time.

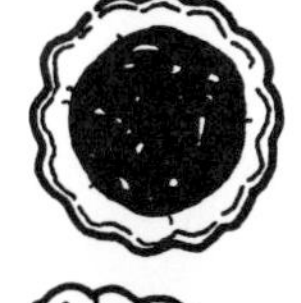

Alice had never been in a court of justice before, but she had read about them in books, and she was quite pleased to find that she knew the name of nearly everything there. "That's the judge," she said to herself, "because of his great wig."

The judge, by the way, was the King; and as he wore his crown over the wig, he did not look at all comfortable, and it was certainly not becoming.

"And that's the jury-box," thought Alice, "and those twelve creatures," (she was obliged to say "creatures" you see, because some of them were animals, and some were birds,) "I suppose they are jurors." She said this last word two or three times over to herself, being rather proud of it: for she thought, and rightly too, that very few little girls of her age knew the meaning of it at all. However, "jurymen" would have done just as well.

The twelve jurors were all writing very busily on slates. "What are they all doing?" Alice whispered to the Gryphon. "They can't have anything to put down yet, before the trial's begun."

"They're putting down their names," the Gryphon whispered in reply, "for fear they should forget them before the end of the trial."

41b Who stole the tarts? (2)

"Stupid things!" Alice began in a loud, indignant voice, but she stopped hastily, for the White Rabbit cried out, "Silence in the court!" and the King put on his spectacles and looked anxiously round, to see who was talking.

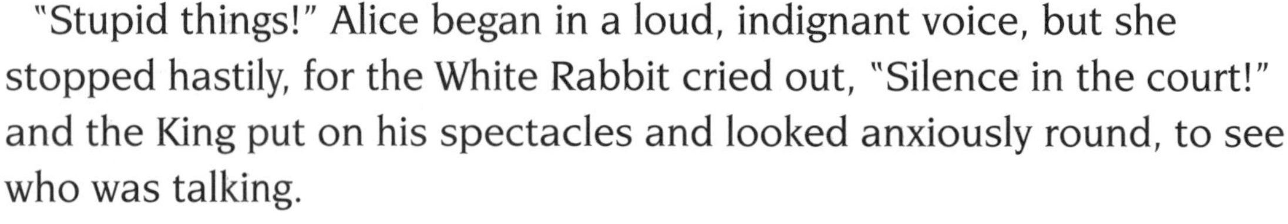

Alice could see, as well as if she were looking over their shoulders, that all the jurors were writing down "stupid things!" on their slates, and she could even make out that one of them didn't know how to spell "stupid", and that he had to ask his neighbour to tell him. "A nice muddle their slates will be in before the trial's over!" thought Alice.

One of the jurors had a pencil that squeaked. This, of course, Alice could *not* stand, and she went round the court and got behind him, and very soon found the opportunity of taking it away. She did it so quickly that the poor little juror (it was Bill, the Lizard) could not make out at all what had become of it…

"Herald, read the accusation!" said the King. On this the White Rabbit blew three blasts on the trumpet, and then unrolled the parchment scroll, and read as follows: –

"The Queen of Hearts, she made some tarts,
All on a summer day:
The Knave of Hearts, he stole those tarts,
And took them quite away!"

"Consider your verdict," the King said to the jury.

"Not yet, not yet!" the Rabbit hastily interrupted. "There's a great deal to come before that!"

"Call the first witness," said the King; and the White Rabbit blew three blasts on the trumpet, and called out, "First witness!"

The first witness was the Hatter. He came in with a teacup in one hand and a piece of bread-and-butter in the other. "I beg your pardon, your Majesty," he began, "for bringing these in but I hadn't quite finished my tea when I was sent for."

From *Alice in Wonderland* by Lewis Carrol

YEAR 4 TERM 1

UNIT **3**

Poetry writing

Learning targets

On completion of this unit children should be able to:

1 ➤➤ compare and contrast poems on similar themes, particularly their form and language, discussing personal responses and preferences

2 ➤➤ write poems based on personal or imagined experience, linked to poems read, list brief phrases and words, experiment by trimming or extending sentences, experiment with powerful and expressive verbs.

Before you start

Background knowledge

This unit leads the children into looking at two poems on a similar theme which is treated in a very different way, eliciting a very different response from the reader. Session 1 gives the children the opportunity to read, discuss and express preferences, Session 2 to write poems of their own. The structure of this unit can be adapted to any poems of your choice.

Resources for Session 1

Copymaster 42 The Snare, Copymaster 43 I Saw a Jolly Hunter, Copymaster 44 Reynard the Fox.

Resources for Session 2

Copymaster 45 Spiders! pencils.

Links to other units

Learning Targets: Reading and Writing Key Stage 1 Section 1 Unit 1 on rhyme, Unit 5 on narrative poetry and Unit 6 on descriptive poetry.

Assessment indicators

- Can the children recognise the point of view of a poet about his/her subject?
- Can they write poetry on the same subject from different points of view?
- Can they express and justify their preferences?

Teaching the sessions

Session 1

Introduction

30min

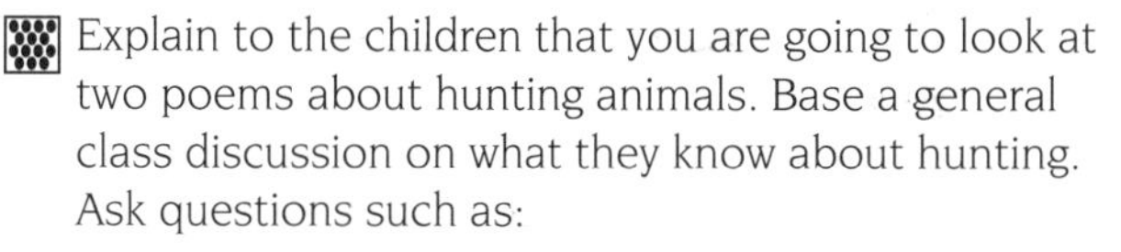

Explain to the children that you are going to look at two poems about hunting animals. Base a general class discussion on what they know about hunting. Ask questions such as:

- 'Why do people hunt?'
- 'What sort of animals are hunted?'
- 'What are they hunted for?'
- 'How do the children feel about hunting animals?'
- 'Have they ever been involved in a hunt?'

The discussion may broaden into animals hunting animals for food or protection, etc. How is this the same or different to when humans hunt animals?

At this point give each child **Copymaster 42 The Snare**. Read it through with the children and discuss:

1 the storyline of the poem

2 the rhyme scheme

3 how they feel when they have read the poem

4 how they think the poet wanted them to feel.

Give each child **Copymaster 43 I Saw a Jolly Hunter**, and repeat the activity. Look closely at the vocabulary in each poem and ask the children what effect it has on them.

The Snare	I Saw a Jolly Hunter
cry of pain	jolly hunter
calling out for aid	walking in the country
frightened air	jolly meadow
afraid	took jolly care
his paw is in the snare	

The poet's point of view

20min

Put the children into groups and ask them to discuss each poem in turn in terms of:

- what the poet thinks about hunting
- what the poet wants the reader to think about hunting
- how each poet has written about the subject.

Both poets are anti-hunting and want the reader to be anti-hunting.

James Stevens' poem is serious and tragic. He makes the reader aware that the rabbit is in pain and afraid. He makes us feel horrified that this is happening to the animal.

Charles Causley has written a humorous poem. We know the hare takes care when it sees the hunter but we never feel it is afraid. Even though the hunter dies, it is written in such a way that we find it amusing to think he shot himself rather than the hare.

Summary

10min

The children can compare their thoughts about the poems through class discussion.

Reynard the Fox

20-25min

Give the children **Copymaster 44 Reynard the Fox** and explain that you want them to read the poem to themselves and then answer the questions. It is important, from time to time, that children engage with poetry individually to assess their level of comprehension and their personal response.

Homework

When the children have finished their individual work, read the poem to them, emphasising the sense of urgency the poem transmits. Ask them to imagine, whilst you are reading, that they are the fox being chased. For homework, the children can write briefly about their feelings. Giving their reasons, they should say whether they like/dislike the poem.

- 'How do they feel about the fox and the hunters?'
- 'How do they think the poet wants them to feel?'

Session 2

Introduction

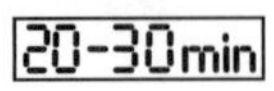

20-30min

Write the following on the board:

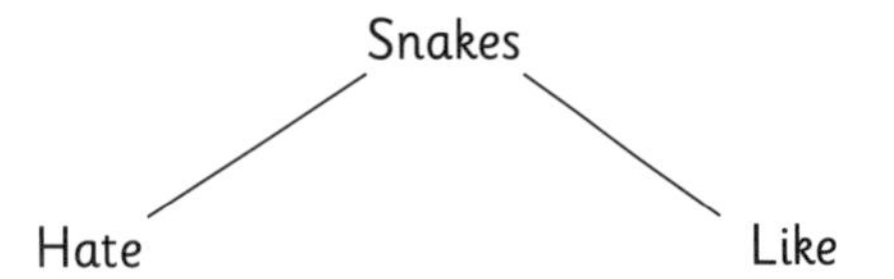

Explain to the children that you are going to write two poems about snakes. In the first one you dislike snakes and you want your reader to dislike them too. In the second poem you like snakes and you want your reader to feel the same way.

Ask the children to help you compile a list of words and phrases on the board that they would use if they liked snakes. Repeat the activity with words and phrases they would use if they *disliked* snakes. The children will probably have little difficulty with the 'Hate' column but they will have to think hard about the 'Like' column.

The lists can be used as the basis for two class poems which can begin:

Snakes	Snakes
We hate snakes	We like snakes

While the class is composing the poems, pay particular attention to the following areas.

1. Some children will suggest whole sentences, e.g. 'I hate snakes because they are cold and slimy'. Use this opportunity to highlight how sentences can be trimmed to capture the essential point, e.g.

   Snakes
   I hate snakes
   Cold and slimy

2. Ask the children if they can expand any of the words in the lists by adding another word beginning with the same letter or sound to make alliterative phrases, e.g.:

   fierce fangs
   glides gracefully
   horrible hiss

3. Can the children use the words and phrases to make similes to describe the snake?

   spits like fire
   fangs as sharp as knives
   coils like a rope

Spiders

20min

Working in groups give each child **Copymaster 45 Spiders!** The children should complete the first section of the copymaster based on group discussion. The second half will be completed on an individual basis. Be on hand to help the children trim sentences, and use alliterative phrases and similes.

Summary

10min

The children can share their ideas through class discussion and add to their lists.

Spider poems

20min

Each child should write two spider poems from opposing points of view. Remind the children that they must remember how they want their readers to feel.

Homework

The children can complete their poems for homework and illustrate them. They can then be used for display.

The Snare

I hear a sudden cry of pain!
 There is a rabbit in a snare:
Now I hear the cry again,
 But I cannot tell from where.

But I cannot tell from where
 He is calling out for aid;
Crying on the frightened air,
 Making everything afraid.

Making everything afraid,
 Wrinkling up his little face,
As he cries again for aid;
 And I cannot find the place!

And I cannot find the place
 Where his paw is in the snare;
Little one! Oh, little one!
 I am searching everywhere.

James Stevens

I Saw a Jolly Hunter

I saw a jolly hunter
With a jolly gun
Walking in the country
In the jolly sun.

In the jolly meadow
Sat a jolly hare.
Saw the jolly hunter.
Took jolly care.

Hunter jolly eager –
Sight of jolly prey.
Forgot gun pointing
Wrong jolly way.

Jolly hunter jolly head
Over heels gone.
Jolly old safety-catch
Not jolly on.

Bang went the jolly gun.
Hunter jolly dead.
Jolly hare got clean away,
Jolly good, I said.

Charles Causley

Reynard the Fox

The fox was strong, he was full of running,
He could run for an hour and still be cunning,
But the cry behind him made him chill,
They were nearer now and they meant to kill.
They meant to run him until his blood
Clogged on his heart as his brush with mud,
Till his back bent up and his tongue hung flagging,
And his belly and brush were filthed with dragging.
Till he crouched stone-still, dead-beat and dirty,
With nothing but teeth against the thirty.

John Masefield

1 How would you describe the fox at the beginning of the poem?

____

____

2 What is happening to the fox? ______________________________

____

3 What 'cry' do you think the fox hears behind him? ______________

____

4 What happens to the fox when he hears that cry? ______________

____

5 What will the fox look like when he has stopped running? ________

____

6 How do you think the poet wants you to feel about the fox? ________

____

7 What do you think happens to the fox? ______________________

____

45 Spiders!

Words and phrases to use if you don't like spiders	Words and phrases to use if you do like spiders

Now write your poems.

Spiders
I hate spiders

Spiders
I like spiders

Historical stories

Choose one of the characters above.

Write a character sketch.

Here are some things to think about.

1 Do you want your reader to like or dislike your character?

2 What does your character look like?

3 What sort of person is your character?

Play scripts

Read the following extract. Write it as a play script, remembering:

- the scene
- the characters' names
- stage directions
- dialogue.

"What are we going to do now?" whispered Peter.
"I don't know!" hissed Kate.
It was very dark in the cave now that Kate had dropped the torch.
"I'll see if I can find the torch," said Peter.
He went down on his hands and knees and felt about carefully on the damp ground.
"Got it!" he cried.
"Sh!" hissed Kate. "Someone will hear us."
"There's no one about to hear us," insisted Peter.

Scene ______________________________

Characters' names	Dialogue/stage directions
______	______
______	______
______	______
______	______
______	______
______	______
______	______
______	______
______	______
______	______
______	______

YEAR 4 TERM 2

Focus

In this section children will be given the opportunity to:

1 investigate/write settings based on imaginary worlds

2 investigate the use of language in old poems and write poetry based on this style of poetry

3 learn basic (editing) skills within the context of imaginary worlds.

Content

Unit 1: Creating imaginary worlds
Unit 2: Poems from long ago
Unit 3: Editing

Reading List

Lewis, C. S. *The Lion, the Witch and the Wardrobe*

Assessment

Assessment Copymasters 57–8 are at the end of the section.

Copymaster 57 Imaginary worlds

Writing composition: gives the children the opportunity to write a description of an imaginary setting based on a picture stimulus.

Copymaster 58 Editing

Writing composition: the children are given a prose paragraph to improve by editing.

National Literacy Strategy planner

This chart shows you how to find activities by unit to resource your term's requirements for text level work on fiction and poetry. The Learning Targets closely follow the structure of the fiction and poetry requirements for the term in the National Literacy Strategy document (pages 40–41). A few of the requirements are not covered. These are usually the ones that require extended reading or writing or comparison of several different texts.

YEAR 4 TERM 2

Range

Fiction and poetry:

- stories/novels about imagined worlds: science-fiction, fantasy adventures
- stories in series
- classic and modern poetry, including poetry from different cultures and times.

TEXT LEVEL WORK

COMPREHENSION AND COMPOSITION

Reading comprehension

Pupils should be taught:

1 to understand how writers create imaginary worlds, particularly where this is original or unfamiliar, such as a science-fiction setting and to show how the writer has evoked it through detail: Unit 1;

2 to understand how settings influence events and incidents in stories and how they affect characters' behaviour: Unit 1;

3 to compare and contrast settings across a range of stories; to evaluate, form and justify preferences;

4 to understand how the use of expressive and descriptive language can, e.g. create moods, arouse expectations, build tension, describe attitudes or emotions: Unit 1 and 3;

5 to understand the use of figurative language in poetry and prose; compare poetic phrasing with narratives/descriptive examples; locate use of simile: Unit 1;

6 to identify clues which suggest poems are older, e.g. language use, vocabulary, archaic words: Unit 2;

7 to identify different patterns of rhyme and verse in poetry, e.g. choruses, rhyming couplets, alternate line rhymes and to read these aloud effectively: Unit 2;

8 to review range of stories, identifying, e.g. authors, themes or treatments;

9 to recognise how certain types of texts are targeted at particular readers: to identify intended audience, e.g. junior horror stories;

Writing composition

Pupils should be taught:

10 to develop use of settings in own writing, making use of work on adjectives and figurative language to describe settings effectively: Unit 1;

11 to write poetry based on the structure and/or style of poems read, e.g. taking account of vocabulary, archaic expressions, patterns of rhyme, choruses, similes: Unit 2;

12 to collaborate with others to write stories in chapters, using plans with particular audiences in mind;

13 to write own examples of descriptive, expressive language based on those read. Link to work on adjectives and similes; Units 1 and 3;

14 notemaking: to edit down a sentence or passage by deleting the less important elements, e.g. repetitions, asides, secondary considerations and discuss the reasons for editorial choices: Unit 3.

YEAR 4 TERM 2

UNIT 1

Creating imaginary worlds

Learning targets

On completion of this unit children should be able to:

1 ➸ understand how writers create imaginary worlds, particularly where this is original or unfamiliar, such as science-fiction settings and to show how the writer has evoked it through detail

2 ➸ develop use of settings in own writing, making use of work on adjectives and figurative language to describe settings effectively

3 ➸ write their own examples of descriptive, expressive language based on those read, link to work on adjectives and similes.

Before you start

Background knowledge

The sessions in this unit deal with settings in imaginary worlds, in both the 'fantasy' and science-fiction genres. The children have the opportunity to invent imaginary worlds by drawing and writing, concentrating on the use of adjectives and similes.

Resources for Session 1

Copymasters 48a–b *The Lion, the Witch and the Wardrobe*, large sheets of paper, crayons, felt-tip pens.

Resources for Session 2

Copymaster 49 Interesting adjectives, Copymaster 50 Similes, pencils, paper.

Links to other units

Learning Targets: Reading and Writing Key Stage 1 Section 2 Unit 3 on setting, Unit 8 on fantasy and imaginary stories

Learning Targets: Grammar and Punctuation Key Stage 1 Section 4, Section 1 of this title (see pages 3–8)

Assessment indicators

- Can the children distinguish between a real world and a fantasy setting?
- Can they write a description of an imaginary setting?

Teaching the sessions

Session 1 ❶ ❷

Introduction

20-30min

By this stage the children will be familiar with including settings in their stories. These will have been, for the most part, descriptions of the 'real world' even though a 'fantastic' element may have entered in the form of a character or event.

Explain to the children that you are now going to look at writing which centres on imaginary worlds. Ask whether the children have any experience of stories like this. Discuss any books they may have read which fall into this category, paying particular attention to the setting rather than the plot. Do the children like these kinds of stories?

Give each child **Copymasters 48a–b *The Lion, the Witch and the Wardrobe*** and read it through with them. Discuss the three distinct stages in Lucy's journey from the real world to the imaginary world.

1 *The real world of the house*
   - 'What impression do the children get of the professor's house?'
   - 'Can they pick out the adjectives and descriptive phrases which say what the inside of the house is like?'

2 *The connection between the real world and the imaginary world, i.e. the wardrobe*
   - 'When does the reader realise there is something odd about the wardrobe?'
   - 'How does Lucy explain to herself the fact that she cannot find the back of the wardrobe?

3 *The imaginary world of the snowy wood*
   - 'What makes Lucy realise that she is no longer in the wardrobe?'

- 'How does Lucy feel when she realises she is no longer in the wardrobe?'

At this point, focus the children's attention on the imaginary world. It is not 'fantastic' or extraordinary in itself: with the exception of the lamp-post in the middle of the wood, the scene is quite ordinary and is a very real world experience.

- 'What makes it so unusual?'
- 'Where do the children think Lucy is?'
- 'Can they think of two reasons why Lucy is only 'a little frightened?'
- 'Do the children think very ordinary things will happen to Lucy or very strange things?'
- 'What sort of characters do they think Lucy will meet?'
- 'Does it remind them of another story where a girl gets into a strange world quite by accident?' (*Alice in Wonderland*)

Through the wardrobe

Working in small groups or pairs, give each group/pair a large sheet of paper. Ask them to imagine that each time someone goes through the wardrobe the imaginary world at the other side is different. The children are going to pretend to go through the wardrobe and draw what the world is like on the other side. Around the edge of their picture they are going to add adjectives and descriptive phrases they would use if they were writing about this other world.

Before they begin to draw, tell them that:

1. their drawings must be different from the world Lucy finds herself in
2. they must decide whether the world they get into is frightening or welcoming.

Be on hand to discuss the 'work in progress' and to ensure that each child has a turn at drawing and annotation.

Summary

10min

Each group/pair can show their drawing and explain:

- what words and phrases they have used
- how they would feel about getting into this world.

My imaginary world

20-25min

Each child should write a short description of the imaginary world 'through the wardrobe' based on their pictures.

Homework

The children can finish the description for homework. These, along with the drawings, can be displayed.

Session 2 ③

Introduction

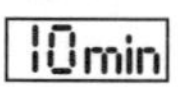

This session concentrates on creating a setting for a story which is based on a far away planet to give the children some experience of one aspect of science-fiction writing.

Explain to the children that two astronauts have landed on a far distant planet which is completely different to our world and that no one has ever visited before. The beginning of the story needs to describe exactly what the astronauts see so that the reader can imagine it in detail. Stress that the astronauts should not meet any 'aliens' at this stage.

Interesting adjectives

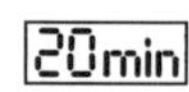

Begin the work in groups with **Copymaster 49 Interesting adjectives**. The children should complete the copymaster and you should be on hand to remind them of the context in which they are working, i.e. the setting for another planet.

Summary

10-15 min

Discuss the children's work, listing really interesting words on the board.

Similes

20min

Another group session can be done with **Copymaster 50 Similes**. You may need to spend some time ensuring that the children have grasped the idea of similes from earlier work.

Stress that they should complete each sentence with an interesting simile that will help the reader to imagine clearly what things look like.

Summary

10-15 min

Discuss the similes the children have written, writing unusual and interesting examples on the board.

Journey to another planet

20-25min

Each child should write the opening to their science-fiction story which describes the scene the astronauts encounter.

Homework

The children can finish their story openings and illustrate them for display.

The Lion, the Witch and the Wardrobe (1)

Peter, Susan, Edmund and Lucy are sent away from London during the war. They go to stay with an old professor who lives in the country. On the first day there it is raining and they cannot go out. They decide to explore the house and this is when Lucy makes an amazing discovery!

Everyone agreed to this and that was how the adventures began. It was the sort of house that you never seem to come to the end of, and it was full of unexpected places. The first few doors they tried led only into spare bedrooms, as everyone had expected that they would; but soon they came to a very long room full of pictures and there they found a suit of armour; and after that was a room all hung with green, with a harp in one corner; and then came three steps down and five steps up, and then a kind of little upstairs hall and a door that led out on to a balcony, and then a whole series of rooms that led into each other and were lined with books – most of them very old books and some bigger than a Bible in a church. And shortly after that they looked into a room that was quite empty except for one big wardrobe; the sort that has a looking-glass in the door. There was nothing else in the room at all except a dead blue-bottle on the window sill.

"Nothing there!" said Peter, and they all trooped out again – all except Lucy. She stayed behind because she thought it would be worth while trying the door of the wardrobe, even though she felt almost sure it would be locked. To her surprise it opened quite easily, and two moth-balls dropped out.

Looking into the inside, she saw several coats hanging up – mostly long fur coats. There was nothing Lucy liked so much as the smell and feel of fur. She immediately stepped into the wardrobe and got in among the coats and rubbed her face against them, leaving the door open, of course, because she knew that it is very foolish to shut oneself into any wardrobe. Soon she went further in and found there was a second row of coats hanging up behind the first one. It was almost quite dark in there and she kept her arms stretched out in front of her so as not to bump her face into the back of the wardrobe. She took a

The Lion, the Witch and the Wardrobe (2)

step further in – then two or three steps – always expecting to feel woodwork against the tips of her fingers. But she could not feel it.

"This must be a simply enormous wardrobe!" thought Lucy, going still further in and pushing the soft folds of the coats aside to make room for her. Then she noticed that there was something crunching under her feet. "I wonder is that more moth-balls?" she thought, stooping down to feel it with her hand. But instead of feeling the hard, smooth wood of the floor of the wardrobe, she felt something soft and powdery and extremely cold. "This is very queer," she said, and went on a step or two further.

Next moment she found that what she was rubbing against her face and hands was no longer soft fur but something hard and rough and even prickly. "Why, it is just like the branches of trees!" exclaimed Lucy. And then she saw that there was a light ahead of her; not a few inches away where the back of the wardrobe ought to have been, but a long way off. Something cold and soft was falling on her. A moment later she found that she was standing in the middle of a wood at night-time with snow under her feet and snowflakes falling through the air.

Lucy felt a little frightened, but she felt very inquisitive and excited as well. She looked back over her shoulder and there, between the dark tree trunks, she could still see the open doorway of the wardrobe and even catch a glimpse of the empty room from which she had set out. (She had, of course, left the door open, for she knew that it is a very silly thing to shut oneself into a wardrobe.) It seems to be still daylight there. "I can always get back if anything goes wrong," thought Lucy. She began to walk forward, *crunch-crunch* over the snow and through the wood towards the other light. In about ten minutes she reached it and found it was a lamp-post. As she stood looking at it, wandering why there was a lamp-post in the middle of a wood and wondering what to do next, she heard a pitter patter of feet coming towards her. And soon after that a very strange person stepped out from among the trees into the light of the lamp-post.

From *The Lion, the Witch and the Wardrobe* by C.S. Lewis

Interesting adjectives

What is there on your planet which you could use these words for?

adjectives

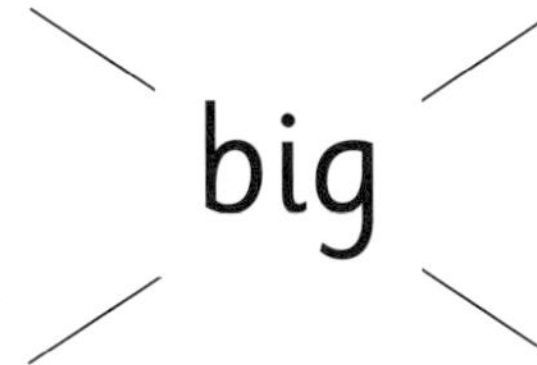

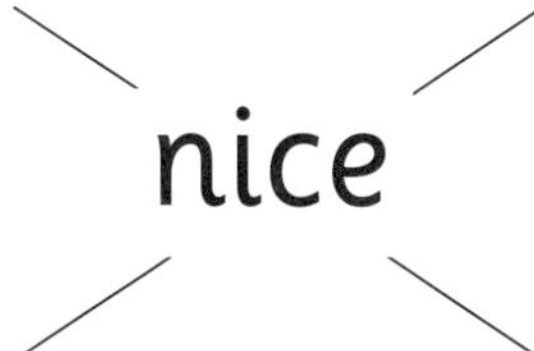

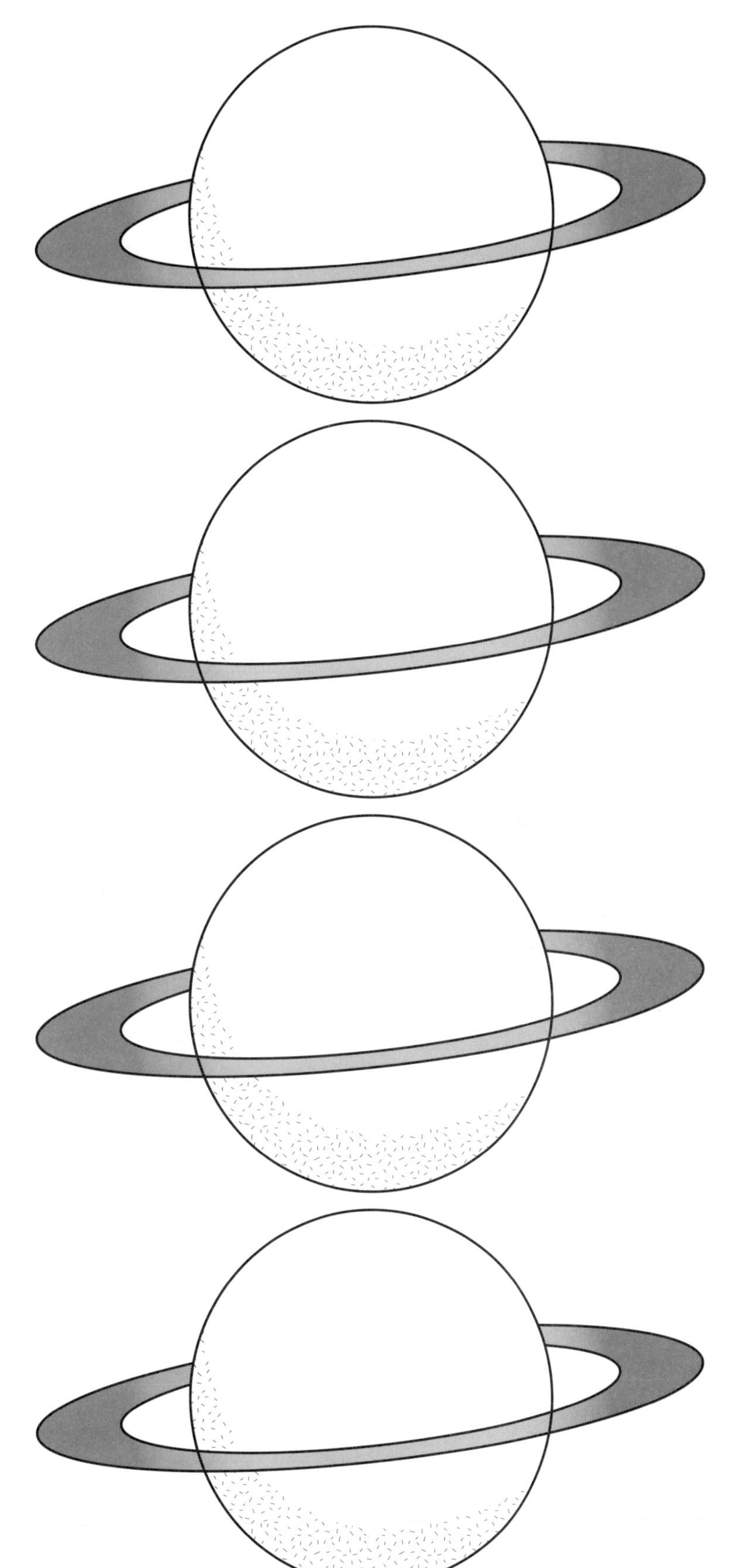

Similes

1 The sky was as ______________________________

as ______________________________ .

2 The rocks were like ______________________________

____

______________________________ .

3 In the sky there were three moons, shining as __________

____

as ______________________________ .

4 The distant mountains were like ______________________________

______________________________ .

5 The leaves on the trees were as ______________________________

as ______________________________ .

6 Many of the flowers which grew there were like __________

____

______________________________ .

YEAR 4 TERM 2

UNIT 2

Poems from long ago

Learning targets

On completion of this unit children should be able to:

1 ➤ identify clues which suggest that poems are older, e.g. language use, vocabulary, archaic words

2 ➤ write poetry based on the structure and/or style of poems read, e.g. taking account of vocabulary, archaic expressions, patterns of rhyme, choruses, similes.

Before you start

Background knowledge

The introduction of older poems can be quite difficult for children of this age so it is wise to use narrative poetry so they can follow a storyline. At Key Stage 1, the children experienced some modern narrative poetry and these sessions build on that knowledge and introduce them to 'older' poems where the verse form and rhyme scheme are familiar but the vocabulary is more challenging.

Resources for Session 1

Copymasters 51a–b King John and the Abbot of Canterbury, Copymaster 52 What do they mean?, pencils, paper.

Resources for Session 2

Copymasters 51a–b King John and the Abbot of Canterbury, pencils, paper.

Resources for Session 3

Copymasters 51a–b King John and the Abbot of Canterbury, pencils, paper.

Links to other units

Learning Targets: Reading and Writing Key Stage 1 Section 1 Unit 5 on narrative poetry

Assessment indicators

- Can the children identify archaic vocabulary and expressions?
- Can they extend an older poem in the same style?

Teaching the sessions

Session 1

Introduction

30min

Begin by asking the children what they understand by narrative poetry. Explain that many narrative poems were written a long time ago and, as such, contain words and expressions that we rarely use today.

Suggest to them that they are going to be detectives and find evidence in the poem you are going to read which will prove that it was written a long time ago.

Give each child **Copymasters 51a–b King John and the Abbot of Canterbury** and read it through with them.

Before looking in detail at the 'evidence', you need to establish that the children have grasped the storyline.

Write the headings 'Characters' and 'Plot' on the board. Ask the children to help you to compile a list of the characters:

- King John
- the Abbot of Canterbury
- the shepherd.

Some of the children might say 'a narrator' but, if not, prompt them by asking what other 'character' you would need if you were going to read this out to the class taking different parts.

Ask the children to help you list the key events.

- The Abbot of Canterbury is summoned to see the King.
- King John wants to know why the Abbot is richer than he is.
- The Abbot says it is all his own money but the king is not pleased.
- The Abbot has to answer three questions or he will be beheaded.
- The Abbot asks for three weeks to come up with the answers.
- He goes to wise men but they cannot help him.
- The Abbot's shepherd says he will go to the King and answer the questions.
- The shepherd answers the questions and the Abbot is saved.

Once you have established that the children understand what is happening in the poem, look at the first verse and ask them to pick out the words that they think show that the poem is an old one. Can they guess at the meanings? E.g.:

anon: shortly
main: force

What do they mean? 15-20min

Put the children into groups and give them **Copymaster 52 What do they mean?** The copymaster is a list of the archaic words/words spelt differently in the poem. Ask the children to discuss them and come up with a modern meaning.

Summary 15min

Compare the children's lists through class discussion.

Session 2 ❶

Introduction 20-25min

Explain to the children that they are going to rewrite some of the poem in modern English so that it could be acted and easily understood today. Ask them to help you put the first verse into modern English, e.g.:

Narrator: This is a very old story about King John. He ruled England with force and he did many wicked things and very few good things.

How would we say it now? 20-30min

Put the children into groups and give them one of the following sections of the play:

Verses 1–10: groups of four children
Verses 11–18: groups of four children
Verses 19–27: groups of three children.

Ask each group to set out their section of the story as a play script, including the narrator if they need one. They should write what the characters say in modern English and use other information from the poem for scene setting and stage directions. They have had experience of turning stories into play scripts in Year 3 but, as this is more tricky, be on hand to discuss the work in progress.

Summary

If time allows, let the children act out their versions of the poem.

Session 3 ❷

Shared writing 20-30min

Explain to the children that they are going to write some more verses for the poem. Can they suggest what they could be about? E.g.:

- 'What might happen the next time King John and the Abbot meet?'
- 'What might the Abbot say to the shepherd when he gets back from seeing the king?'

As this is quite a difficult task, it is best done as a shared writing activity with the whole class, but you could organise this as a group/individual task if you think the children could manage it.

King John and the Abbot of Canterbury (1)

An ancient story I'll tell you anon
Of a noble prince that was called King John;
And he ruled England with main and with might,
For he did great wrong, and maintained little right.

And I'll tell you a story, a story so merrie,
Concerning the Abbot of Canterbury;
How for his housekeeping and high renown,
They rode post for him to fair London town.

An hundred men, the king did hear say,
The abbot kept in his house every day;
And fifty gold chains without any doubt,
In velvet coats waited the abbot about.

"How now father abbot, I hear it of thee,
Thou keepest a far better house than me;
And for thy housekeeping and high renown,
I fear thou workest treason against my crown."

"My liege," quo' the abbot, "I would it were known
I never spend nothing, but what is my own;
And I trust your grace will do me no deere,
For spending my own true-gotten gear."

"Yes, yes father abbot, thy fault is high,
And now for the same thou needst must die;
For except thou canst answer me questions three,
Thy head shall be smitten from thy bodie.

"And first," quo' the king, "when I'm in this stead,
With my crown of gold so fair on my head,
Among all my liege-men so noble of birth,
Thou must tell me to one penny what I am worth.

"Secondlie, tell me, without any doubt,
How soon I may ride the whole world about;
And at the third question thou must not shrink,
But tell me here truly what I do think."

"Oh these are hard questions for my shallow wit,
Nor can I answer your grace as yet:
But if you will give me but three weeks' space,
I'll do my endeavour to answer your grace."

Now three weeks' space to thee will I give,
And that is the longest time thou hast to live;
For if thou dost not answer my questions three,
Thy lands and thy livings are forfeit to me."

Away rode the abbot all sad at that word,
And he rode to Cambridge and Oxenford,
But never a doctor there so wise,
That could with his learning an answer devise.

Then home rode the abbot of comfort so cold,
And he met his shepherd a-going to fold;
"How now, my lord abbot, you are welcome home;
What news do you bring us from good King John?"

"Sad news, sad news, shepherd I must give,
That I have but three days more to live;
For if I do not answer him questions three,
My head will be smitten from my bodie.

"The first is to tell him there in his stead
With his crown of gold so fair on his head,
Among all his liege-men so noble of birth,
To within one penny of what he is worth.

"The second to tell him, without any doubt,
How soon he may ride the whole world about:
And at the third question I must not shrink,
But tell him there truly what he does think."

"Now cheer up, sir abbot, did you never hear yet,
That a fool he may learn a wise man wit?
Lend me horse and serving men, and your apparel,
And I'll ride to London to answer your quarrel.

Nay, frown not, if it hath been told unto me,
I am like your lordship as ever may be;
And if you will but lend me your gown,
There is none shall know us at fair London town."

"Now horses and serving men thou shalt have,
With sumptuous array most gallant and brave,
With crozier and mitre, and rochet and cope,
Fit to appear 'fore our father the pope."

(*Continued*)

51b King John and the Abbot of Canterbury (2)

"Now welcome, sir abbot," the king he did say,
"'Tis well thou'rt back to keep thy day;
For if thou canst answer my questions three,
Thy life and thy living both saved shall be.

"And first, when thou seest me here in this stead,
With my crown of gold so fair on my head,
Among my liege-men so noble of birth,
Tell me to one penny what I am worth."

"For thirty pence our Saviour was sold
Among the false Jews, as I have been told:
And twenty-nine is the worth of thee,
For I think thou art one penny worser than he!"

"The king laughed and swore by St Bittel,
"I did not think I was worth so little!—
Now secondly, tell me, without any doubt,
How soon I may ride this whole world about."

"You must rise with the sun and ride with the same
Until the next morning he rises again;
And then your grace need not make any doubt
But in twenty-four hours you'll ride it about."

"The king he laughed and swore by St John,
"I did not think it could be done so soon!
Now from the third question thou must not shrink,
But tell me here truly what I do think."

"Yes, that I shall do, and make your grace merrie;
You think I'm the abbot of Canterbury;
But I'm his poor shepherd, as plain you may see,
That am come to beg pardon for him and for me."

The king he laughed, and swore by the mass,
"I'll make you lord abbot this day in his place!"
"Now nay, my liege, be not in such speed,
For alack, I can neither write nor read."

"Four nobles a week then I will give thee,
For this merrie jest thou hast shown to me;
And tell the old abbot when thou comest home,
Thou hast brought him a pardon from good
King John."

Anon

What do they mean?

merrie ______________________

rode post ______________________

fifty gold chains ______________________

liege ______________________

deere ______________________

canst ______________________

smitten ______________________

bodie ______________________

stead ______________________

secondlie ______________________

a-going ______________________

apparel ______________________

hath ______________________

shalt ______________________

thou art ______________________

alack ______________________

nobles ______________________

comest ______________________

YEAR 4 TERM 2

UNIT 3

Editing

Learning targets

On completion of this unit children should be able to:

1 ➤➤ make notes, edit down a sentence or a passage by deleting the less important elements – repetitions, asides, secondary considerations – and discuss the reasons for editorial choice.

Before you start

Background knowledge

This unit affords a good opportunity to broaden the scope of the children's 'editing' by highlighting areas where they can improve their written work in a variety of ways:

1 sentence beginnings
2 redundant words
3 replacing overworked words
4 adding interesting details.

When the children have worked through the sessions you can use these four areas of 'editing' so discuss subsequent written work on an individual basis.

Resources for Session 1

Copymaster 53 Sentence beginnings, pencils.

Resources for Session 2

Copymaster 54 Redundant words, pencils.

Resources for Session 3

Copymaster 55 Overworked words, pencils.

Resources for Session 4

Copymaster 56 Interesting details, pencils.

Links to other units

Learning Targets: Grammar and Punctuation Key Stage 1 Section 7 Units 1 and 2

Assessment indicators

- Can the children edit a piece of work in order to improve it?
- Can they edit their own work?

Teaching the sessions

Session 1 ①

Introduction 20–30min

Begin by writing the following sentence on the board:

The sun was shining in the garden although it was late at night.

Explain to the children that too many sentences begin with 'The' or 'I' or 'It was' and this often makes for uninteresting reading. Can they change the order of the words so that 'The' does not come at the beginning?

Although it was late at night, the sun was shining in the garden.

The children should be familiar with the term 'connective/conjunction'. Can they see that it is sometimes possible to begin a sentence with the conjunction to make it more interesting?

Give them some further class practice with the following sentence:

I saw a very strange animal when I was walking to school.
(When I was walking to school I saw a very strange animal.)

It was a bright sunny day until about one o'clock.
(Until about one o'clock, it was a bright sunny day.)

You can also introduce the idea of using a present participle ('ing' word) to begin sentences, e.g.:

I found the key and unlocked the door.
(Finding the key, I unlocked the door.)

I rushed after the old man when I caught sight of him.
(Catching sight of the old man, I rushed after him.)

Sentence beginnings 20min

Give each child **Copymaster 53 Sentence beginnings**, to work through.

Summary 10min

Compare answers through class discussion.

Homework

Choose a piece of writing that the children have already completed and ask them to edit/improve it by changing some of the sentence beginnings.

Session 2

Introduction
10-15 min

Begin by writing the following sentence on the board:

He walked through the door and he walked over to the fire.

Can the children suggest a way to improve this sentence? Can they see that some of the words are not necessary?

He walked through the door and over to the fire.

Write the following example on the board:

'What time is it?' he shouted loudly.

Can the children see which word is unnecessary in this sentence? 'Loudly' is not needed as, if you shout, then it will be loud.

The children can have fun suggesting sentences with unneccessary words and improved versions.

Unnecessary words
10-15 min

Give each child **Copymaster 54 Unnecessary words**, to work through.

Summary
10min

Compare answers through class discussion.

Homework

Using the same piece of writing the children worked on for Session 1 Homework, ask them now to improve it by removing any unneccessary words.

Session 3

Introduction
20min

Write 'overworked words' on the board and ask the children what sort of words they think these are. Through their suggestions, they should come to the conclusion that these are words which are used too often and, as such, don't really help a reader to picture clearly what is being written about. You could also lead them into seeing that they are 'general' words and, by using more precise words, their writing will be more interesting.

Ask the children to give you some examples of words that are 'overworked'. The most common ones are:

got said big nice little

Use these as headings on the board and spend some time compiling lists of alternative/more interesting/precise words for the children to draw on in their individual work.

Overworked words
10-15 min

Give each child **Copymaster 55 Overworked words**, to work through.

Summary
10min

Compare answers through class discussion.

Homework

The children should look at their piece of writing again to substitute interesting words for any 'overworked' words they have used.

Session 4

Introduction
20min

Explain that an important way to improve writing is to add details which will give the reader a clearer picture. Draw on the work they have done on adjectives and adverbs in this session. Can they remember what job these words do?

Write the following sentences and questions on the board:

We had to climb the mountain.

What sort of mountain?

Ask the children to suggest what the mountain might look like.

high rugged frightening gigantic

Holly jumped over the fence.

How did she jump?

Ask the children *how* Holly jumped.

energetically clumsily nimbly quickly

This activity can be repeated with various sentences which lack adjectives and adverbs.
Point out that sentences can be improved by adding a phrase, e.g.:

Holly jumped over the fence as quickly as she could.

Adding interesting details
25min

Give each child **Copymaster 56 Adding interesting details,** to work through.

Summary
10min

Compare answers through class discussion.

Homework

The final edit of the children's pieces of writing should concentrate on adding details for interest.

53 Sentence beginnings

Rewrite the sentences so that they begin with a conjunction or an 'ing' word.

1 The spaceship landed in the garden while I was having my tea.

2 I hid around the corner and watched the strange creatures get out of the spaceship.

3 The spaceship took off with a loud roar.

4 I didn't come out of my hiding place although the creatures seemed friendly.

5 They walked over to the garden shed and went inside.

Unnecessary words

Rewrite the sentences, leaving out the unnecessary words.

1 "Don't make a noise," she whispered quietly.

2 Did you buy any fruit when you did the shopping at the shops?

3 She rushed into the room very quickly.

4 "I don't like and hate sprouts!" shouted Tim.

5 When you go to town will you go and get a newspaper for me?

Overworked words

Rewrite these sentences, replacing the underlined words with more interesting words.

You may have to change other words as well.

1 What have you got in your hand?

____

____

2 "I'm very frightened," said Harry.

____

____

3 The elephant is a big animal.

____

____

4 That meal was very nice.

____

____

5 The giant towered above the little houses.

____

____

Adding interesting details

Improve these sentences by adding descriptive words that show:

a what something looks, sounds or feels like

b how an action is done.

1 The creature came out of the cave.

2 The sea was blue.

3 Sam walked along the road.

4 The clouds moved across the sky.

5 There was a noise in the forest.

Imaginary worlds

This picture looks like an ordinary wood but it is far from ordinary. Everything about it is very different to any wood you will ever go into. Imagine this wood is the setting for your story. Write a description of it, making it as strange as you can!

Editing

Edit/improve this piece of writing.

The big wolf went down to the little river to drink. There were no other animals there and he felt safe as he was by himself on his own. The wolf had a drink and sat down to rest.

A bear walked out of the trees. The bear roared. The wolf got up and ran away. The bear went down to the river. He walked across the river. The wolf looked out of the trees. He looked to see if the bear had gone. He went back down to the river and sat down.

YEAR 4 TERM 3

Focus

In this section children will be given the opportunity to:

1 investigate/write stories which deal with problems, concentrating on characters' behaviour

2 investigate/write various forms of poetry, e.g. alphabet poems, list poems, number poems, etc.

Content

Unit 1: Stories raising issues
Unit 2: Poetic forms
Unit 3: Syllabic poetry

Reading List

Cotton, John 'First Things'

Doherty, Berlie 'White Water'

English, Anne 'Birds in the Garden'

McGough, Roger 'First Haiku of Spring'

Swindells, Robert *The World Eater*, Hodder & Stoughton, 1991

Assessment

Assessment Copymasters 70–72 are at the end of the section.

Copymaster 70 Stories dealing with issues

Writing composition: this gives the children a planning sheet for initial notes on a story where the main character has a problem.

Copymaster 71 Syllabic poems

Writing composition: this sheet gives the children writing frames and suggestions for a 'growing' poem and a 'diamond' poem.

Copymaster 72 Haiku and cinquain

Writing composition: this sheet provides a framework for two kinds of syllabic poems.

National Literacy Strategy planner

This chart shows you how to find activities by unit to resource your term's requirements for text level work on fiction and poetry. The Learning Targets closely follow the structure of the fiction and poetry requirements for the term in the National Literacy Strategy document (pages 42–3). A few of the requirements are not covered. These are usually the ones that require extended reading or writing or comparison of several different texts.

YEAR 4 TERM 3

Range

Fiction and poetry:

- short stories/novels, etc. which raise issues, e.g. bullying, bereavement, injustice
- stories by the same author
- range of poetry in different forms, e.g. haiku, cinquain, lists, thin poems, alphabets, conversations, monologues, syllabic, prayers, epitaphs, songs, rhyming forms and free verse.

TEXT LEVEL WORK

COMPREHENSION AND COMPOSITION

Reading comprehension

Pupils should be taught:

1 to identify social, moral or cultural issues, e.g. the dilemmas faced by characters or the moral of the story, and to discuss how the characters deal with them; to locate evidence in text: Unit 1;

2 to read stories from other cultures, by focusing on, e.g. differences in place, time, customs, relationships; to identify and discuss recurring themes where appropriate;

3 to understand how paragraphs or chapters are used to collect, order and build up ideas;

4 to understand the following terms and identify them in poems: verse, chorus, couplet, stanza, rhythm, alliteration: Unit 2;

5 to clap out and count the syllables in each line of regular poetry: Unit 3;

6 to describe how a poet does or does not use rhyme, e.g. every alternate line, rhyming couplets, no rhyme, other patterns of rhyme;

7 to recognise some simple forms of poetry and their uses, e.g. the regularity of skipping songs, the chorus in songs: Unit 2;

8 to write critically about an issue or dilemma raised in a story, explaining the problem, alternative courses of action and evaluating the writer's solution: Unit 1;

9 to read further stories or poems by a favourite writer, making comparisons and identifying familiar features of the writer's work;

10 to describe and review own reading habits and to widen reading experience;

Writing composition

Pupils should be taught:

11 to explore the main issues of a story by writing a story about a dilemma and the issues it raises for the character: Unit 1;

12 to write an alternative ending for a known story and discuss how this would change the reader's view of the characters and events of the original story: Unit 1;

13 to write own longer stories in chapters from story plans;

14 to write poems, experimenting with different styles and structures, discuss if and why different forms are more suitable than others: Units 2 and 3;

15 to produce polished poetry through revision, e.g. deleting words, adding words, changing words, reorganising words and lines, experimenting with figurative language: Units 2 and 3.

YEAR 4 TERM 3

UNIT **1**

Stories raising issues

Learning targets

On completion of this unit children should be able to:

1 ➤ identify social, moral or cultural issues in stories, e.g. the dilemmas faced by characters or the moral of the story, and to discuss how the characters deal with them; to locate evidence in the text

2 ➤ write critically about an issue or dilemma raised in a story, explaining the problem, alternative courses of action and evaluating the writer's solution

3 ➤ explore the main issues of a story by writing a story about a dilemma and the issues it raises for a character.

Before you start

Background knowledge

The emphasis of these sessions is on moral dilemmas rather than physical ones. Session 1 is based on an extract where a character is a loner who is bullied by his classmates and not really understood by his mother. Session 2 invites the children to consider various problems they may have faced or might face in the future and to use one of these situations as the basis for a story of their own.

Resources for Session 1

Copymasters 59a–b *The World-Eater*.

Resources for Session 2

Copymaster 60 Solving problems, pencils, paper.

Links to other units

Learning Targets: Reading and Writing Key Stage 1 Section 2 Unit 7 on traditional stories

Assessment indicators

- Can the children identify a problem faced by a character in a story and suggest ways of dealing with it?
- Can they construct a story around a character in a difficult situation?

Teaching the sessions

Session 1 ① ②

Introduction 20-25min

Give each child **Copymasters 59a–b *The World-Eater***, and read it through with the children. Base a class discussion on the following, to ensure they have grasped what is happening.

- 'What happened during the night?'
- 'What happened to Mr McDougal's house?'
- 'Where did Mr McDougal go the next morning?'
- 'Why was Mum so interested in listening to the news on the radio?'
- 'What did Orville do before he had breakfast?'
- 'What was Orville going to have to do because Mr McDougal had gone away?

The important part of the extract centres on Orville's hobby and his relationships with his mother and the other children at school. Discuss these issues with the children:

- 'How does Orville's mother feel about the pigeons?'
- 'What would she rather Orville spent his time doing? Why?'
- 'What "problem" does Orville have?'
- 'How is he treated by the other children at school?'
- 'Why is he friendly with Mr McDougal rather than with people his own age?

Lead the children into seeing that Orville is 'different'. He doesn't like doing the things boys of his age normally like.

Discuss how he is treated at school.

- 'Why is he treated like this?'
- 'Is it fair?'
- 'Is it reasonable to make fun of someone who is different or likes to do different things?'

Discuss how Orville felt when he tried to talk about his hobby at school.

- 'Would the children have felt the same?'
- 'Would they have refused to go on talking?'
- 'Could Orville have reacted differently?'
- 'What could he have done?'

How would it feel? 30min

Put the children into groups of five so that one can be Miss Jenner, one Orville and three, children in the class. Explain that they are going to act the scenes from the story where:

1 Orville tries to give his talk on his hobby
2 Orville is made fun of in the playground.

You will need to monitor this carefully as there may be a tendency for some children to want to do just the 'tripping up' part! Explain to the children that what they must concentrate on is how they 'feel' while they are 'in character', and that you will be discussing these feelings after they have acted the scenes. The children will need to invent some of the dialogue, e.g. how Miss Jenner begins the lesson, what she says when the children make fun of Orville, the beginning of Orville's talk on pigeons, etc.

Go around the groups as they are working and talk about their 'character'.

Summary

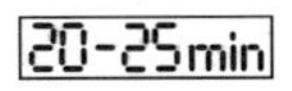

Discuss each of the characters in turn with the children who played the part.

Miss Jenner:

- 'How were you feeling at the beginning of the lesson?'
- 'Were you worried about Orville giving his talk?'
- 'Did you think it would be all right?'
- 'How did you feel when some of the class started to laugh?'

Orville:

- 'How did you feel about having to talk about the pigeons?'
- 'Were you looking forward to it?'
- 'How did you feel when some of the class started to laugh?'
- 'Did you feel angry/upset/embarrassed?'
- 'Why did you go and sit down?'

The others:

- 'Do you like/dislike Orville?'
- 'Were you interested in what he had to say?'
- 'Did you enjoy making him upset?'
- 'Did you feel sorry for him at any time?'
- 'Did you try to imagine what it would be like in Orville's situation?'

How I felt

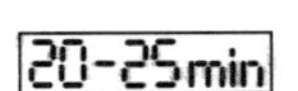

Ask the children to write about their part in the 'play', concentrating on:

1 why they acted as they did
2 how they felt about what they did.

Homework

The children can continue with their individual work at home.

Session 2

Introduction

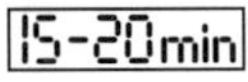

Recap on the extract from Session 1, discussing the 'problem' that Orville had: being 'different' and being bullied because of it. Can the children think of any other problems which they have faced or might have to face? Situations might include bereavement, knowing that someone has done something wrong and having to decide whether to 'tell' or not, being blamed for something they haven't done.

Explain that many stories include characters who face these kind of problems. Sometimes a reader will agree with how a character deals with a problem, and sometimes not. It may be possible at this stage to extend the discussion to consider some of the stories the children have read where a character or characters have faced a problem and how they dealt with it. Some children may recount incidents from stories where a character has been frightened or in danger. Are these the same sorts of 'problems'? Can the children distinguish between these sorts of problems and the one Orville faced?

Solving problems

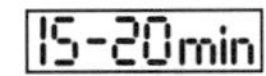

Put the children into groups and give each group **Copymaster 60 Solving problems**. Ask them to discuss each one in turn and make notes to answer each question. Stress that they can consider various ways of behaving rather than just one course of action.

Summary

10-15 min

As a class, discuss the different solutions that each group found.

Problems in stories

30min

Ask the children to choose one of the situations from Copymaster 60 Solving problems and write a story about it. It is important that the reader knows how the character who has the problem feels and how the other characters react.

Homework

The children can finish their stories for homework.

The World-Eater (1)

One night there is a terrible storm. A young boy called Orville is woken up and goes to his window to watch the storm. He sees a neighbour, Mr McDougal, standing outside looking at Orville's window. Orville calls his father and they bring Mr Mc Dougal inside. He tells them that a huge tree has fallen on his house and he has seen something 'strange' in the sky. Orville and Mr McDougal are good friends because they both keep pigeons.

Here is part of the story from the morning after the storm.

It was late when he woke up. He got up and looked out of the window. The storm had died down. There was rubbish everywhere; tins and paper and broken glass, but the loft was still there. He dressed quickly and went downstairs.

His mother was sweeping the step. He stuck his head outside. 'Dad gone to work, Mum?'

'Hours ago. It's after ten.' She went on sweeping. It was glass, from milk bottles.

'Where's Mr McDougal?'

'Gone to stay with his sister. Dad took him on the way to work. Get the dustpan, please.'

They cleared away the glass. After, he went across to the loft. Susie was all right and the others seemed much as usual, too. He let them out to fly, fed them, then went in for some late breakfast. His mum was ironing and listening to the radio.

'Mum?'

'Ssh!' She was listening to the news. Orville shrugged and went on with his cornflakes. After a minute his mum said, 'Hear that, Orville?'

'What?'

'Listen. It says they had storms all over the world. Worse than here. Earthquakes and that. Listen.'

The World-Eater (2)

Orville listened, but the man was on about Bosnia. His mum made an impatient sound. 'You missed it, chomping on those cornflakes. Earthquakes, and dams bursting and tidal waves and that. It's the headlines. We'll have to listen at eleven.'

'Did it say anything about what Mr McDougal saw?'

'No.' His mother's tone was scornful. 'He didn't see anything, the daft so-and-so.' Orville sighed but did not argue. It was no use arguing.

He finished his cornflakes and got up. 'I'll have to do his pigeons as well as mine,' he said. 'They've not been fed.' He crossed to the door.

His mother shook her head. 'You and your pigeons. Why don't you play football in the park or something, like other boys?'

He stopped, reluctantly. 'Don't like football, Mum.' He didn't like other boys much, either. They laughed at him because of his name. They laughed because of the pigeons, too.

Once, in Miss Jenner's class, he'd stood out at the front and started telling them about his pigeons. They were doing about hobbies. When he said 'Doridins,' they started to titter, and when he mentioned 'Cattryses' they laughed, and big daft Cowling at the front rolled about, whooping 'Cattryses' in a high voice. Miss Jenner was blazing mad and shouted at them to be quiet. When they were, she wanted him to continue but he couldn't. He felt hot and dizzy and he knew if he tried to speak he'd cry. So he just shook his head and went back to his place and sat very stiff, looking down.

Afterwards, in the yard, they got him. They crowded round him and pushed him about with their shoulders, saying 'Cattryse' and 'Doridin' and 'Pigeon-pie' until he couldn't hold it in any more and started to cry. Then they jeered and tripped him up and left him on the ground. It was a while ago now, but he still went hot when he thought of it.

'Oh, well.' His mother's voice broke in on his thoughts. 'I suppose if you were a footballer I'd grumble about your getting dirty or something. Off you go. And keep away from that tree; it's not safe.'

From *The World Eater* by Robert Swindells

Solving problems

1 Your friend's dog has died and he/she is very upset. What would you do and say in this situation?

2 Your friends want to play a trick on an old lady who lives in your street. How do you feel about what they want to do?

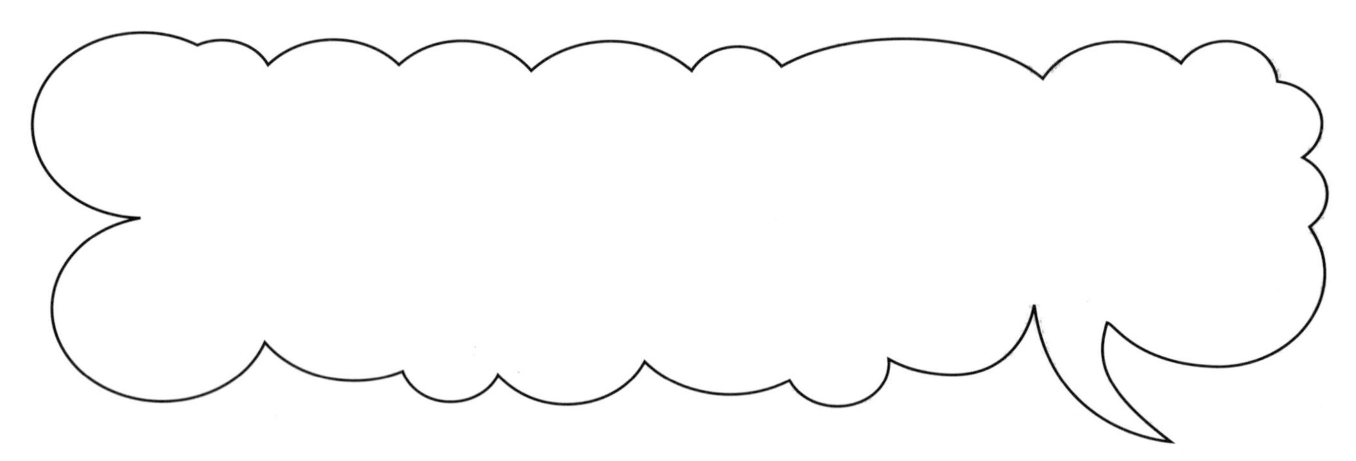

3 You have been accused unfairly of breaking a window at school. What would you do and say in this situation?

YEAR 4 TERM 3

UNIT 2

Poetic forms

Learning targets

On completion of this unit children should be able to:

1 ➛ recognise some simple forms of poetry and their uses

2 ➛ write poems, experimenting with different styles and structures, discuss whether and why different forms are more suitable than others.

Before you start

Background knowledge

This unit deals with using lists as poems and takes the children from single object word lists, lists as activity poems and descriptive poems, through to number list poems.

Resources for Session 1

Card, felt-tips, hole punch, string.

Resources for Session 2

A picture depicting a busy scene, Copymaster 61 Underwater, pencils.

Resources for Session 3

Copymaster 62 First Things, Copymaster 63 Likes and Dislikes, pencils, paper.

Resources for Session 4

Copymaster 64 Number poems, flashcards, pencils, pens.

Links to other units

Learning targets: Reading and Writing Key Stage 1 Section 1 Unit 4 on acrostics and Unit 6 on descriptive poetry

Assessment indicators

- Can the children recognise a 'list' poem in various forms?
- Can they write their own list poems using alliteration?

Teaching the sessions

Session 1 ① ②

Introduction 20-30min

Begin by asking the children to help you compile object lists on the board, e.g.:

- five things you have in your school bag
- five things you like to eat.

The children may reply in sentences, e.g. 'I like to eat chips.' Slim these down to the bare essentials so you end up with a list like this:

Eating
Chips
Apples
Ice-cream

See if the children can make some of the list alliterate, e.g.:

Eating
Carrots
Cucumbers
Cream
Crackers

The lists can be extended by pairs of words beginning with the same letter, e.g.:

Eating
Chips and chops
Bread and butter
Apples and artichokes
Dripping and damsons

By rearranging the lines you have an alphabetical, alliterative list poem:

Eating
Apples and artichokes
Bread and butter
Chips and chops
Dripping and damsons.

Making lists 20-30min

Let the children experiment with making object lists, writing single words, pairs of alliterative words and rearranging them to form an alphabet poem.

When the children have finished, they can write their poems on card and hang them up as mobiles. The card could be cut into the shape of one of the objects in their poem.

Summary 10min

Some of the children may like to read their poems to the class.

Session 2 ① ②

Introduction 20-25min

Recap on object list poems from the previous session and explain to the children that you can write list poems which are descriptive. Display the poster and ask the children to say what they see, e.g. a jungle scene:

Darting birds
Hunting tiger
Tall trees
Chattering monkeys

Explain to the children that they are still compiling a list of objects but they are using adjectives to extend their poem.

Making descriptive lists 30min

Let the children experiment with descriptive list poems based on the poster. These can be displayed around the poster.

Give the children **Copymaster 61 Underwater**, to write a descriptive list poem about. Let them colour the picture and use the copymasters for display.

Summary 10min

Some of the children might like to read their poems to the class.

Homework

The children can finish their copymasters at home.

Session 3 ① ②

Introduction 20-30min

Recap on the descriptive list poems from the previous session and explain to the children that you can make list poems about things you do. Give each child **Copymaster 62 First Things**, and read it through with the children. Can they see that the poem is a list of things which the poet likes to do?

Give each child **Copymaster 63 Likes and Dislikes**, and read it through with the children. How is it similar to 'First Things'? How is it different? Can the children see that the repetition of '-ing' words gives the poem its rhythm?

Descriptive list poems 30min

Ask the children to write either a 'First Things' poem or a 'Likes and Dislikes' poem. Explain that the 'First Things' poem does not have to rhyme although the one on the copymaster does. It can be a list of 'first things' they particularly like or dislike but they should try to use phrases rather than single words.

Summary 30min

Some of the children might like to read their poems to the class.

Session 4 ① ②

Introduction 20-25min

Explain to the children that numbers are very useful in writing list poems. Give each child **Copymaster 64 Number poems**, and read the poems through with the children. How are the poems similar? How are they different? They should comment on the repetition in the first poems and the use of alliteration in the second.

Do the children know any number poems? They may give examples of poems or chants that are used in playground games. Do they know 'Ten Green Bottles'?

Ask the children to help you compile an alliterative number list poem on the board. Use the numbers five to ten so they do not merely repeat the adjectives used on the copymaster and begin by asking for adjectives that begin with the same letters, e.g.:

five	fierce	floppy
six	silly	super
seven	simple	sunny
eight	eager	empty
nine	naughty	nice
ten	tall	tame

Choose an 'object' that the poem is to be about and ask the children to select the most suitable adjectives for each number.

One, two, three 30min

Each child should now attempt a number poem of their own. They can choose their own 'object' or you could take out the nouns from a set of flashcards, lay them face down on the desk and let the children choose from those. They can use some of the adjectives on the board but they should try to think of as many new ones as possible.

Summary 30min

Some of the children might like to read their poem to the class.

Underwater

Underwater I can see...

First Things

The first lick of the lolly,
The first bite of the cake,
There is something about them
You cannot mistake.

The first day of the holidays,
The first time you wear
Something new, then that feeling
So special is there.

The first time you open
A new comic the smell
Of the ink and the paper
Is exciting as well.

The very first bike ride,
The first dip in the sea,
The first time on a boat
Were all thrilling to me.

The first page of a book,
The first words of a play,
And the first thing in the morning
When you start a new day.

John Cotton

Likes and Dislikes

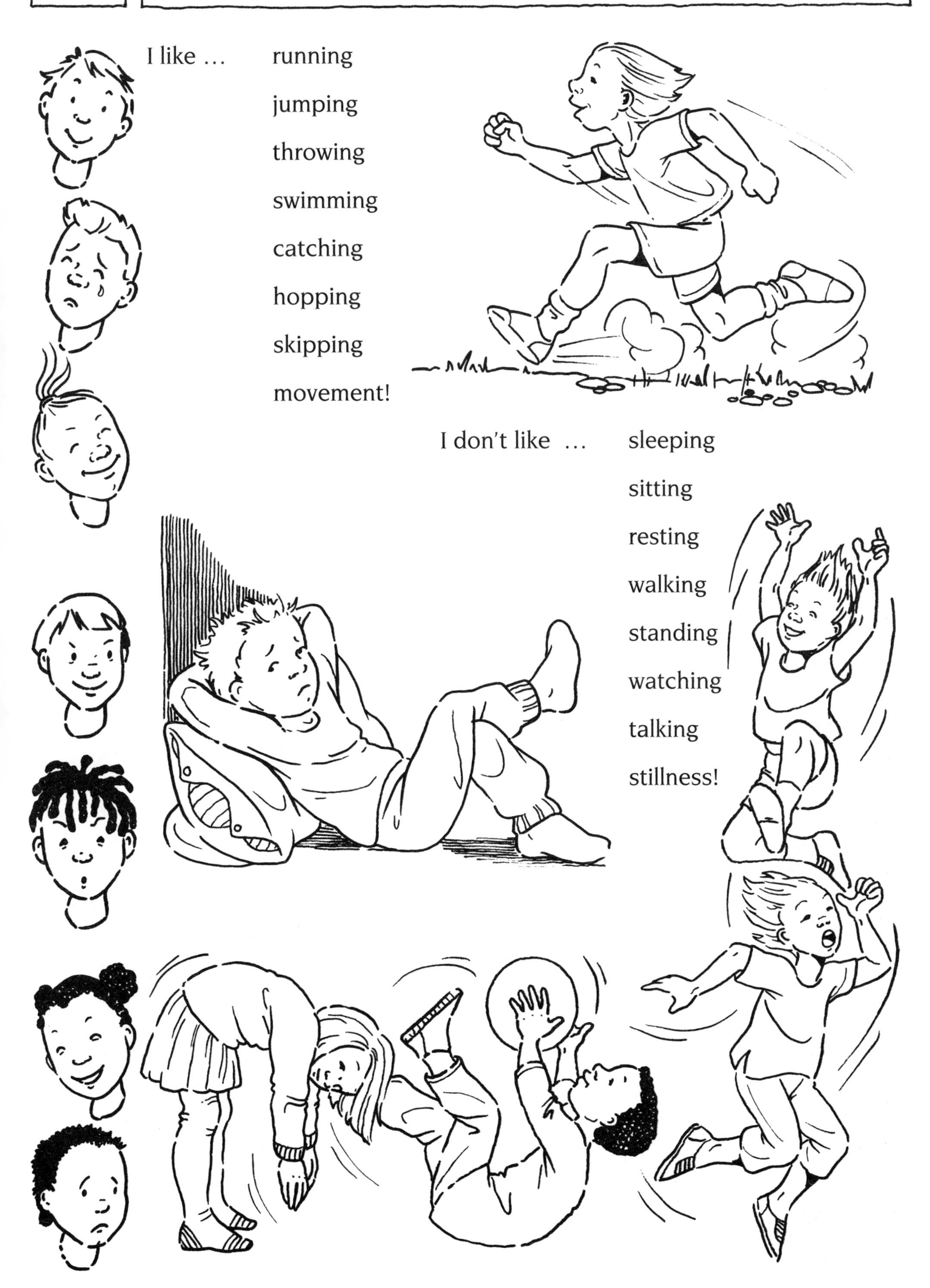

I like ... running
jumping
throwing
swimming
catching
hopping
skipping
movement!

I don't like ... sleeping
sitting
resting
walking
standing
watching
talking
stillness!

Number poems

Birds in the Garden

Four birds sat in a row
Waiting for the peas to grow.
One bird flew away,
Said he'd come back another day.

Three birds sat in a line
Waiting for the sun to shine.
One bird flew away,
Said he'd come back another day.

Two birds sat together
Waiting for the rainy weather.
One bird flew away,
Said he'd come back another day.

One bird sat on his own.

Rain came,
Sun hot,
Peas ripe,
He gobbled the lot.

Anne English

Birds

Four fluffy, feathered birds,
Three thirsty, thin birds,
Two tiny, timid birds,
One odd, old bird.

YEAR 4 TERM 3

UNIT 3

Syllabic poetry

Learning targets

On completion of this unit children should be able to:

1 ➤ recognise some simple forms of poetry and their uses

2 ➤ write poems, experimenting with different styles and structures.

Before you start

Background knowledge

This unit is linked to the previous one and extends the form and structure of poetry on which the children can model their own writing. Sessions 1 and 2 give the children the opportunity to experiment with syllables and syllabic poems in preparation for Sessions 3 and 4 where haiku and cinquain poetry are introduced.

Resources for Session 1

A file, ruler, magazine, dictionary, Copymaster 65 Words on a theme, pencils.

Resources for Session 2

Copymaster 66 Syllable poems, pencils, paper, felt-tip pens.

Resources for Session 3

Copymaster 67 Haiku, Copymaster 68 Writing haiku.

Resources for Session 4

Copymaster 69 Writing cinquains, pencils, felt-tip pens.

Assessment indicators

- Can the children recognise syllables in words?
- Can they use syllables to write various forms of poetry?

Teaching the sessions

Session 1 ①

Introduction 30 min

It is important to spend some time ensuring that the children are comfortable with the idea of syllables in words. Place the file, ruler, magazine and dictionary on the desk. Pick up the things in order and say the name, stressing the syllables. Ask the children to name something that could go in the 'file' group. Through accepting a suggestion, e.g. 'pen', and rejecting others, e.g. 'pencil' some of the children will get the idea. Go through all the objects like this and then ask the children why some things can be grouped together and some not.

Write these headings on the board:

1 syllable   2 syllables   3 syllables   4 syllables

Ask the children to think of words which can go under each heading. They must give you the word and say where you should write it.

Introduce the idea of counting syllables in phrases to add to your list, e.g.:

a 2–syllable phrase: I saw
a 3–syllable phrase: a hedgehog
a 4–syllable phrase: I was running

Words on a theme 15–20 min

Put the children into groups of four and give each group **Copymaster 65 Words on a theme**. Ask the children to write as many words and phrases as come to mind for each 'theme' in the correct list.

Summary 10 min

The children can compare the syllabic words and phrases through class discussion.

Keep the completed copymaster for the next session.

Session 2 ① ②

Introduction 20 min

Explain to the children that they are going to use the work they have done on syllables to write 'growing poems' and 'diamond poems'. Give each child **Copymaster 66 Syllable poems**, and read it through with them.

Discuss how each poem is structured. 'Birds' and 'The Old Man' are 'growing' poems: each line has an extra syllable.'Chips' and 'Snow' are 'diamond' poems: each poem begins and ends with a one-syllable word.

Writing syllable poems
20-30min

Give the children their completed Copymaster 65 and ask them to choose one of the themes they have written words and phrases about. Using this work they can write a 'growing' or a 'diamond' poem. They should be encouraged to work in draft, copy up neatly and illustrate their work for display.

Session 3
① ②

Introduction
20min

Explain to the children that they are going to use what they have learned about syllables and syllable poems to write a special kind of poem called a 'haiku'. They may be interested to know that this is a form of traditional Japanese poetry which is structured in the following way:

1st line: five syllables

2nd line: seven syllables

3rd line: five syllables.

Give each child **Copymaster 67 Haiku** and read through the poems with the children. They should find 'The First Haiku of Spring' quite amusing but they should begin to realise by reading the others that a haiku captures and describes moments in time.

The first haiku is like a photograph of the birds as they sit together, huddled up on a cold morning.

'White Water' is really a series of haiku, each one describing an aspect of the scene, i.e. canoes, voices, heron, the moon.

Writing haiku
20-25min

Some children will have little difficulty in writing this kind of poetry but for those who find it quite a challenge, **Copymaster 68 Writing haiku**, will provide some support. Emphasise that the lines are for syllables, not words.

Encourage the children to think of something interesting to write about, perhaps beginning with an observation in the classroom. Be on hand to suggest words they could use, as once children have a word in mind which does not fit the syllabic pattern, it can be quite difficult for them to reject the word and search for another.

Summary
10min

Some of the children might like to read their poems to the class.

Homework

The children can copy their haiku and illustrate it for display.

Session 4
① ②

Introduction
20-30min

The work on haiku can be extended into looking at another form of poetry which depends on syllabic regularity know as the 'cinquain'. It was devised by an American poet called Adelaide Crapsey.

Explain to the children that the cinquain has a pattern of syllables as follows:

1st line: two syllables
2nd line: four syllables
3rd line: six syllables
4th line: eight syllables
5th line: two syllables

This is obviously more challenging than the haiku and it is a good idea to compose a class cinquain before the children write individually. Brainstorm a particular topic for the poem by asking the children for words and phrase that come to mind, e.g.:

winter
holidays
a sport
an animal

Write their suggestions on the board and then the structure of the poem in the form of lines.

1st line ___ ___

2nd line ___ ___ ___ ___

Remind the children that each line represents a syllable, not a word.Use the words and phrases to compose the poem.

Writing cinquains
20-30min

As with haiku, some children will cope whilst other will need support. **Copymaster 69 Writing cinquains**, will provide a structure for some children.

Summary
10min

Some of the children may like to read their poems to the class.

Homework

The children can copy their cinquain and illustrate it for display.

65 Words on a theme

A Winter's Day

1 syllable

2 syllables

3 syllables

4 syllables

Eating ice-cream

1 syllable

2 syllables

3 syllables

4 syllables

Syllable poems

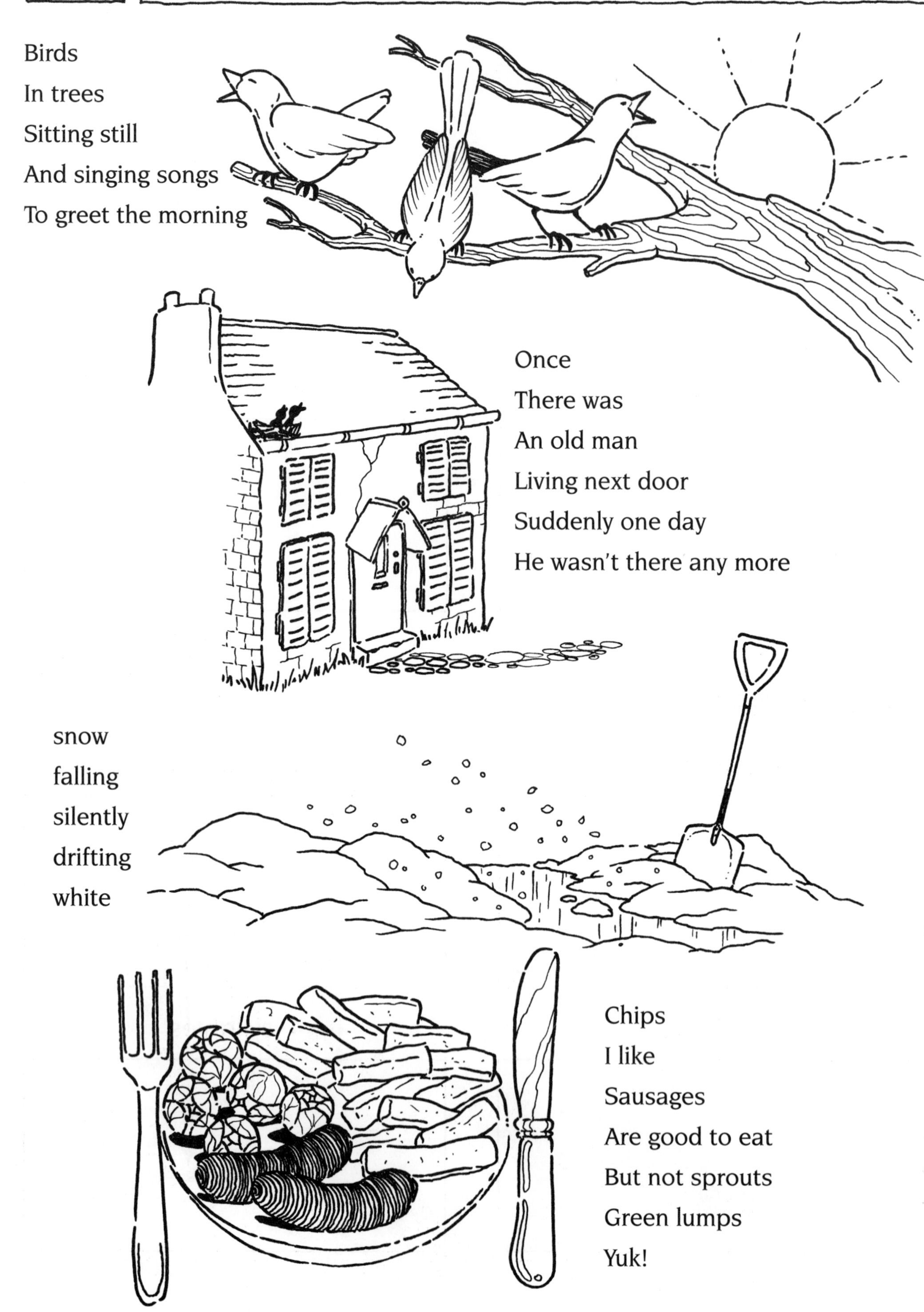

Birds
In trees
Sitting still
And singing songs
To greet the morning

Once
There was
An old man
Living next door
Suddenly one day
He wasn't there any more

snow
falling
silently
drifting
white

Chips
I like
Sausages
Are good to eat
But not sprouts
Green lumps
Yuk!

Haiku

A bitter morning
sparrows sitting together
without any necks.

J W Hackett

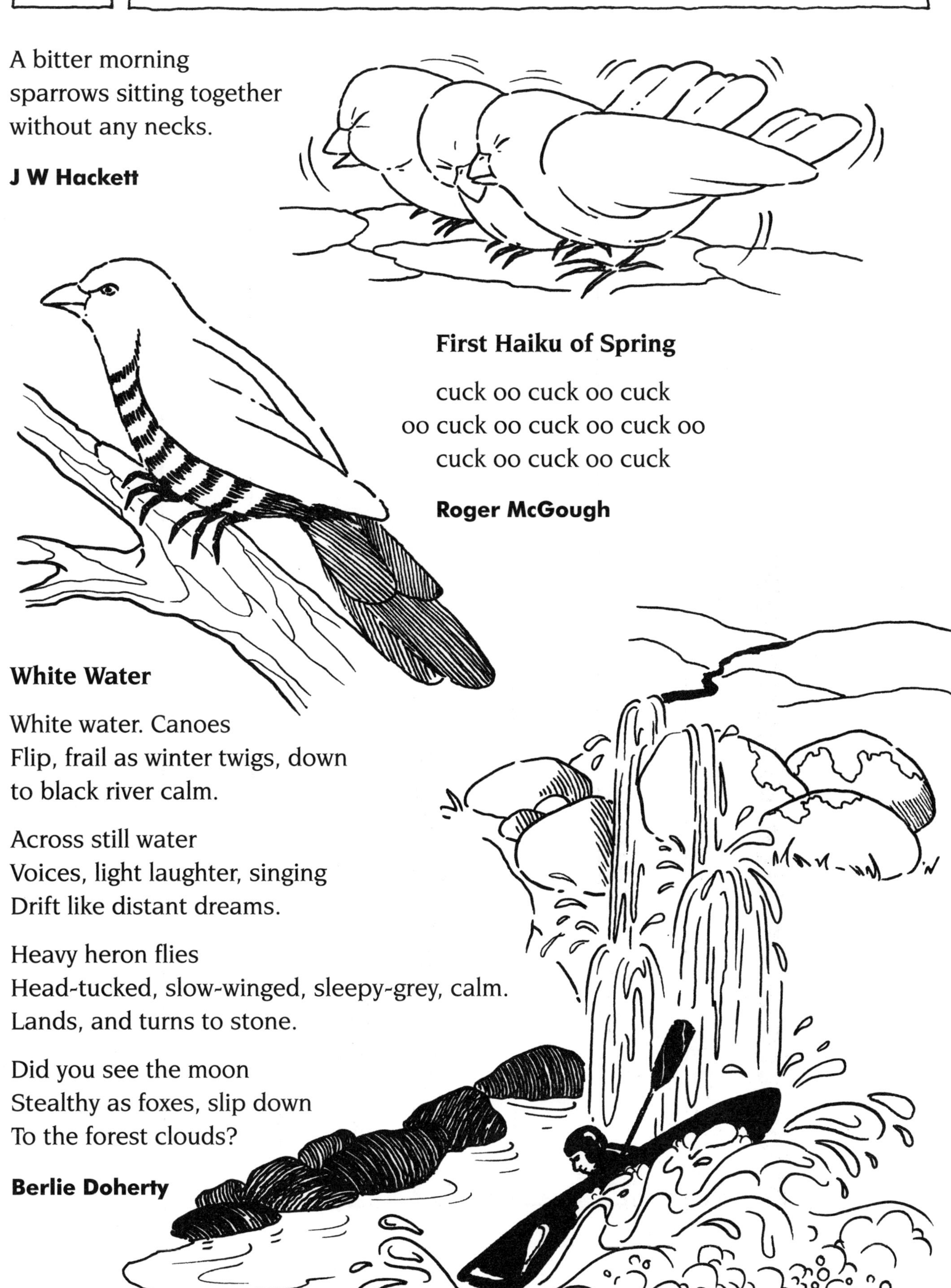

First Haiku of Spring

cuck oo cuck oo cuck
oo cuck oo cuck oo cuck oo
cuck oo cuck oo cuck

Roger McGough

White Water

White water. Canoes
Flip, frail as winter twigs, down
to black river calm.

Across still water
Voices, light laughter, singing
Drift like distant dreams.

Heavy heron flies
Head-tucked, slow-winged, sleepy-grey, calm.
Lands, and turns to stone.

Did you see the moon
Stealthy as foxes, slip down
To the forest clouds?

Berlie Doherty

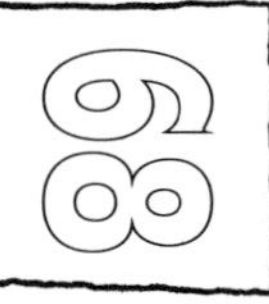

Writing haiku

Working in the classroom

A boy is _____ _____

His friend paints _____ _____ _____ _____

I _____ _____ _____ .

Out of the window

Look ing _____ _____ _____

I see _____ _____ _____ _____ _____

Trees _____ _____ _____ _____

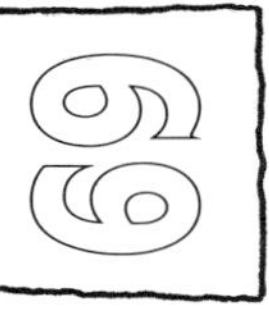

Writing cinquains

Playing football

Foot ball

Can be ___ ___

Kick ing ___ ___ ___ ___

Run ning ___ ___ ___ ___ ___ ___

___ ___

Playing in the sand

Dig ging ___ ___

Build ing ___ ___ ___ ___

Shells and ___ ___ ___ ___ ___ ___

___ ___

70 Stories dealing with issues

Plan and write a story where the main character has a problem and has to solve it. For example the character might:

- be being bullied
- have no friends
- have done something wrong and is worried and frightened.

Use this planning sheet to make notes before you begin to write.

Main character

The problem

How the problem is solved

Other characters in the story

Where the story takes place

71 Syllabic poems

1 Write a 'growing' poem about an animal.
Remember that each black line is a syllable, not a word.

1st line ________

2nd line ________ ________

3rd line ________ ________ ________

4th line ________ ________ ________ ________

2 Write a diamond poem about a means of transport.
Remember that each black line is a syllable, not a word.

1st line ________

2nd line ________ ________

3rd line ________ ________ ________

4th line ________ ________ ________ ________

5th line ________ ________ ________

6th line ________ ________

7th line ________

72 Haiku and cinquain

1 **Write a haiku about the rain.**

Remember that each black line is a syllable not a word.

1st line ____ ____ ____ ____ ____

2nd line ____ ____ ____ ____ ____ ____ ____

3rd line ____ ____ ____ ____ ____

2 **Write a cinquain about yourself.**

Remember that each black line is a syllable, not a word.

1st line ____ ____

2nd line ____ ____ ____ ____

3rd line ____ ____ ____ ____ ____ ____

4th line ____ ____ ____ ____ ____ ____ ____ ____

5th line ____ ____